# WRITING THE EASY WAY

Charlene
Frazier

# WRITING THE EASY WAY

## FOR
## SCHOOL, BUSINESS, AND
## PERSONAL SITUATIONS

by

**Phyllis Dutwin**
Vice President
Reading and Educational
Services, Inc.
East Greenwich, Rhode Island

and

**Harriet Diamond**
President, Diamond Associates,
Human Resource Development Consultants
Westfield, New Jersey

## BARRON'S EDUCATIONAL SERIES, INC.
Woodbury, New York · London · Toronto · Sydney

*All inquiries should be addressed to:*

Barron's Educational Series, Inc.
113 Crossways Park Drive
Woodbury, New York 11797

Library of Congress Catalog Card No. 85–7357

International Standard Book No. 0–8120–2729–9

Library of Congress Cataloging in Publication Data

Dutwin, Phyllis.
  Writing the easy way.

  Bibliography: p.
  1. English language—Rhetoric.   2. English
language—Grammar—1950–       I. Diamond, Harriet.
II. Title.
PE1408.D87     808′.042     85–7357
ISBN 0–8120–2729–9

PRINTED IN THE UNITED STATES OF AMERICA
 678  100  98765432

## Acknowledgments

The authors are grateful to the following copyright owners for allowing them to reprint portions of their works in this book:

American Phonemeter Corp., for the paragraph on page 86, from their 1982 Annual Report.

Consumers Union, Inc., for the paragraph on page 83, adapted from "Sunscreens," *Consumers Reports* June 1983.

Burrows, William E., for the paragraph on page 81. First appeared in *Science Digest* ©1983 by The Hearst Corporation.

Davis, William S., for the paragraph on page 87, from *BASIC: Getting Started,* © 1981. Published by Addison-Wesley Publishing Company.

Smithsonian Books, for the paragraph on page 82, from *Thread of Life.* © 1982 by Smithsonian Institution Press.

*Whodunit? A Guide to Crime, Suspense and Spy Fiction,* H. R. F. Keating, Editor. Compilation copyright © 1982 by H. R. F. Keating. All rights reserved.

# Table of Contents

# Introduction

Because you care about your appearance, you comb your hair, wear clean clothes, and keep your shoes in good repair. These aspects of your appearance are part of the image you want to project. Your writing also projects an image of yourself. Be sure it represents you well. Each time you send a letter, write a memo, or hand in a term paper, you're on display. If the material leaves your desk before you've styled the sentences and corrected any grammar and usage errors, you risk appearing sloppy and uneducated. So take the time to groom your writing.

Business managers frequently complain that employees don't know how to write. When an employee sends a report or memo, they say, it often confuses rather than informs. It often has to be rewritten or followed up with telephone explanations, which take yet more time. Managers complain that they are spending too much of their time correcting employees' written work. It angers and frustrates them, because they are using time they need to do more creative jobs.

But business managers aren't the only people who complain about the quality of writing today. Teachers say that students have problems expressing their understanding of a subject, simply because they can't write about the subject. How many students have lost out on a higher grade — or even failed a course — because although they knew the subject matter, they couldn't properly answer an essay question or prepare a term paper?

Even when writing is a personal matter between family members or friends, or a letter of instructions to a repairman, or a complaint to a department store, your writing will represent you. If your letter is sloppy or your meaning unclear, you risk making the wrong impression — or not getting what you want.

What does this mean for you? Everything. A person who can communicate well is much more likely to be hired, to earn better grades, to have his or her wants understood. If you can write well, you are more likely to succeed at whatever you want to do.

# How Can This Book Help?

When you were young, you were taught many things, but you probably never were taught *how* to write. For example, if, by the time you reached the fifth grade you were still adding a column of 5's to find out how much seven of them equalled, a teacher would have insisted that you learn the multiplication tables. You would have been shown a procedure for calculating the answer in a short time. You probably suffered a bit while you learned to multiply, but afterwards you had a process that cut your working time while giving you more confidence and less pain.

This book is designed to help you get your thoughts on paper. "Stop!" you say. "I don't even have the thoughts to put on paper. Can you help me, too?" You do, in fact, have thoughts to put on paper, but when confronted with a blank sheet, those thoughts often retreat. Relax; you are not alone. *Writing the Easy Way* is designed to help you combat the "empty paper syndrome" with tips on collecting those thoughts and arranging them in a meaningful way.

Many people — even professional writers — experience problems with their writing. The editors of *Writers Digest* asked several authors to write about how they go about writing. In a humorous vein, Stanley Ellin, author of *Dreadful Summit* and the *Eighth Circle,* proves the point. He talks first about the wonderful books he's written — in his head — followed by the "glowing mental reviews" of his imagined work. And then Mr. Ellin continues:

> So much for the good news.
> The bad news is that there always seems to come a day when I must descend to reality and actually put some of those words on paper. And, in so doing, must recognize yet again that I was born with a faulty connection between mind and hand, something which suggests that I've been thinking those marvelous tales in Venusian, a language notoriously untranslatable into English . . .
> Eventually, I will write a page. Then I will study it with the horrified realization that, as all good things must, an otherwise promising literary career has just come to an abrupt end . . .

Len Deighton, author of *Goodbye to Mickey Mouse* and *XPD*, said:

> . . . the difficulty of saying anything about writing is that each writer has to find a way to winkle material out of his own brain. Furthermore, each book has different problems that need to be tackled in a new way.

My own writing is characterized by an agonizing reappraisal of everything I write so that I have to work seven days a week and usually do an hour or so even on Christmas Day, simply to keep all the problems fresh in my mind.

The most difficult lesson to learn is that thousands and thousands of words must go into the waste paper basket. To soften the blow, I place scrapped chapters on a high shelf before tossing them away.

Here's another comment, this one from Eric Ambler, author of *The Pair of Time* and *The Mask of Dimitrios*:

> The fun begins — and in the beginning stages it is all fun — when I start to work this thing out on paper. There will be many false starts and long pauses for reflection . . .
>
> Generally, the pauses can be measured in days. And all the time I'm gradually discovering what the story I have embarked upon is about. However, I am not yet committed. I can still scrap the 50 or 60 pages of writing and rewriting that may have by then accumulated and turn to something else . . .

In case you are wondering if any of this applies to you — after all, you don't write fiction — it does. Whether you write fiction or fact, you are dealing with two actions: creating (a spontaneous, uncorrected flow of writing) and revising (a careful editing of writing).

*Writing the Easy Way* will teach you how to reduce the time it takes to write (create and revise) and, in so doing, will help rid you of some of the frustration. If you don't like the way you write, if writing is a painful process, stop blaming yourself. Stop suffering. Learn to write, THE EASY WAY.

# 1.

# Thinking Before You Write

---

Whatever you intend to write, whether it be a letter or a term paper, one thing is certain. You should make some important decisions before you get started. You could delay making those decisions — as many people do — and end up writing your piece again and again until you hit upon what you want to say. Or you could do some critical thinking *before* you write, and save yourself a great deal of time and frustration. Which way is better? Try our way this time and see if you like the results.

## Some Basic Questions

What are the questions you should ask yourself before you write? Let's consider them, and see how the answers to them will make your writing easier.

### Should I Write?

If you can accomplish your purpose by talking to someone, then talk! During your work day, if you see an associate three, four, perhaps five times, there may be no need to write a memo regarding a simple matter. Say what you want if the issue can be concluded with that conversation, and save time and paper. However, don't expect a busy co-worker to carry your request in his or her head for an hour, a day, or a week. Do yourself and the person with whom you are communicating a favor. Write the question, give the information, or make the request you want. If you don't commit your request or message to paper, the person receiving it will have to remember it or write it down. You risk having your message ignored or forgotten.

If you are a homeowner with a complaint about the broken street light on your corner, your request to the Village Hall will get faster attention if it arrives on paper. And if you are a student with an assignment to write a term paper, of course you have no choice but to put your thoughts down on paper. The teacher wants to know how well you have learned your subject, but also wishes to see how effectively you organize that information and convey it to another person. When you write, you must make those thoughts clear to your reader. Thus, for many instances, you will have to write your message, and you want that message to be understood.

## Who Is My Reader?

You can't move any closer to writing itself until you determine who will read what you write. Who your audience is will determine what type of writing you will do. Think of one idea going to two different people. For example, the following two letters describe a job, first to a friend, then to a potential employer. Notice how Jane's tone changes, depending on whether she is writing to someone she knows well or a potential employer.

Dear Judy,

I've finally decided to pack in this dead-end job. I can no longer calmly listen to Mr. B. present my ideas as his accomplishments. He is so convinced they're his, he even brags to me about them. Most recently, I developed a training program for new employees. I sent him a draft. A week later, a manual was circulated with his name on it. He didn't even correct my typing error. I've applied for a comparable position in another company and hope to have good news for you soon.

Love,
Jane

16 Sunset Road
Boise, Idaho 83701
April 3, 1985

Ms. Eunice Munson
General Manager
ABC Corporation
Boise, Idaho 83720

Dear Ms. Munson:

I am writing in response to your ad in Sunday's *Inquirer* for an assistant manager. I believe my experience is directly related to the position offered.

For the past five years, I have assisted the manager of XYZ Corporation. My duties have included drafting speeches, devising company manuals, and providing administrative support. Most recently, we worked together on a training manual for new employees. While I still find my present position challenging, I am seeking employment with greater growth potential.

I enclose a copy of my resumé and look forward to hearing from you at your earliest convenience.

Sincerely,
Jane Brody

Each time you are going to write something, ask yourself: Do I know the reader? Picture in your mind the person or group you are addressing. If your picture is clear, you can focus your writing on that person's interests or needs. Consider your reader's relationship to you (relative, friend, colleague, teacher) and his or her familiarity with the subject. These considerations will affect the words you choose and the manner in which you express your thoughts.

### What Do I Want to Say?

If you've reached this point, you probably know what you want to say — whether you are writing a letter to your Congressperson or a book report for your teacher. We discuss purpose in greater detail in the following chapter, because recognizing what you feel and think can still be worlds apart from understanding the "purpose" of your writing. For example, you may feel angry that the dress you bought shrunk when you washed it, but the purpose of your writing a letter to the store will be to persuade them to give you your money back. For now, you should consider your basic motivation in writing. Are you going to berate your Senator for voting against the Clean Air Bill or will you congratulate him for his veto? Will your term paper support the idea that Hamlet had a tragic flaw or will it show him as a victim of circumstance? Before you write, you must know what you want to say.

### How Do I Say it Best?

Writing takes many forms: letters, memos, reports, notes, lists, and books, to name just a few. Depending on your intention, the form you choose will determine the structure of your writing. We discuss the forms of writing in greater detail in Chapter 5.

## Formal and Informal Writing

We've discussed some basic questions you should ask yourself before you begin writing. If you've been thinking about who your reader is, then you've moved along to another fundamental aspect of writing: the levels of language. Usually we don't think much about language levels because most of the time we automatically choose the correct level for our purpose. Language, however, can be either formal or informal, depending on the choice of words, the arrangement of sentences, and the overall tone and structure. Both levels are correct when used at the appropriate time, but you should recognize the differences and know when to use each.

Writing to a friend, you would never say,

> Dear Thomas Grey:
> I received your note of June 18, 1984, which inquired about my health. Please be advised that the flu has passed and I have returned to work . . .

Too formal! However, you would say,

> Dear Tom,
> Thanks for your note. Yes, I had a terrible two weeks battling the flu, but I'm back at work now and feeling fine . . .

What are the differences between these two letters? What makes one formal and the other informal? Write your opinion on a sheet of paper and then compare it to the answer key at the end of the chapter.

## More About Levels of Writing

If you were writing a letter to a prospective employer, you would *not* say:

> It was really great hearing from you. Sure, I'll come in for my second interview on December 22, 1983. I'll see you at about 9:00 A.M. Thanks again . . .

If you were serious about getting that job, you would write in a more formal style:

> Thank you for scheduling a second interview. I look forward to seeing you on December 22, 1983 at 9:00 A.M. . . .

"Formal," however, does not mean stilted. Avoid words and phrases that are stiff and arduous, making you seem like a stuffed shirt. How would you react to this letter, and what impression would it leave?

> May I express my deep gratitude on having received your request for a second interview. You certainly can rely upon my arrival at your office promptly at 9:00 A.M.

Each time you write or speak, you choose — consciously or unconsciously — the level of language you want. You didn't have to read this book to know that the first version — the informal one — sounds wrong considering the occasion and the reader. Did you know, though, that being informal does not always mean being incorrect? Used at the right time, an informal approach allows you to communicate in a more conversational way, perhaps getting your idea across in a friendly, effective way. The conversational tone may be extremely light, as in the letter to Tom, or less so, as in this book.

Which of the following three notes might the president of a major corporation write to one of his salesmen whose wife just gave birth to a boy?

> Dear John:
> Congratulations to you and Maria on the birth of John, Jr. I know you will have many proud and happy years ahead.
> Sincerely,
> William Gilbert

> Dear John,
> Way to go! My best to you and Maria. There will be many times in the years to come when you and I will be raising our mugs for John, Jr.
> Best wishes,
> Bill

> Dear Mr. Stillman:
> I wish to extend my heartfelt congratulations to you and Mrs. Stillman on the birth of your son, John, Jr. I look forward to sharing your pride on future occasions.
> Sincerely,
> William Gilbert

The first is the best for this situation; it is formal, but friendly. The second is unquestionably too informal; it would more likely be sent to a very close friend. The third choice is stilted, and inappropriate when the reader and writer know each other well.

## PRACTICE 1

When do you write in a formal tone? When would informal language be more suitable? You make the decision.

Listed below are *occasions*. Rate each occasion **F** for Formal or **I** for Informal.

| | Occasion | Formal or Informal? |
|---|---|---|
| 1. | A cover letter for your résumé. | F |
| 2. | A toast to your good friend on his 50th birthday. | I |
| 3. | A letter to your lawyer about a suit for damages. | F |

4.    A thank-you note to your
      grandmother.                          _____ I _____

5.    A research paper for
      your psychology class.               _____ F _____

# Informal, Not Substandard

An informal level of writing is not the same as a substandard level. Substandard English is incorrect, no matter who the reader or listener, and includes faulty grammar, awkward sentence structure, and incorrect word usage. For example, it is unacceptable to say, "My foreman *don't* ever give me credit for good work," even if you're writing to your mother. Always follow the rules of standard written English.

**PRACTICE 2**

Test your understanding of the differences between informal and substandard language. As you read each sentence, decide if it contains informal or substandard (incorrect) language. Check the appropriate box.

1.   Here's the user manual you asked for.
                     ___✓___ Informal    _____ Incorrect
2.   Our department hardly never takes time for lunch.
                     _____ Informal    ___✓___ Incorrect
3.   Neither Smith nor Jones are ready to report.
                     _____ Informal    ___✓___ Incorrect
4.   It's never too early for a coffee break.
                     ___✓___ Informal    _____ Incorrect
5.   Glancing down the darkened street, the trees were a haven for muggers.
                     _____ Informal    ___✓___ Incorrect

# Special Language

One of the first questions discussed in this book was "Who is my reader?" We mentioned that knowing who your reader is will help you set the tone of your writing. You should also ask yourself what your reader already knows about the subject. What information does he or she bring to the material? This is a critical question, especially when you're writing technical material. Don't risk annoying your reader by making him or her work too hard. Use language that is appropriate to your reader's level of understanding.

Sometimes the simple addition of a few words will make the sentence clearer. Suppose you had to explain the forms of computer documentation. You might write this:

> *TUT-DOCs* include one or more tasks for the user to perform.

Your reader may understand this if he or she is familiar with computer documentation. If your reader is not, the addition of four words clarifies the sentence;

> *TUT-DOCs* are tutorial statements, lessons that include one or more tasks for the user to perform.

How effective do you think the following memo is in conveying the important information?

> TO: All New Employees
> FROM: Director of Employee Benefits
>
> Please have all appropriate information regarding your EBP in my office before the payroll due date of this month. This should include FWT, BCBS, and MM data.

To all new employees? Do they know the payroll due date? Are they familiar with all of the abbreviations? Do they know what the appropriate information is? The writer of this memo would have saved time and subsequent explanatory phone conversations if he took more time to write a clearer memo:

> TO: All New Employees
> FROM: Director of Employee Benefits
>
> Please have the following information regarding your Employee Benefits Program in my office by March 20, 1985, the payroll due-date of this month:
>> Name
>> Address
>> Social Security number
>> Previous insurance policy number and carrier
>> Number of dependents
>> Names, ages, and birthdates of other members of your family to be included in insurance coverage.
>
> This information is required for either federal withholding tax, Blue Cross/Blue Shield, or Major Medical insurance coverage.

## PRACTICE 3

Decide if each writing sample that follows is too formal, too informal, or just right for the occasion or purpose. Rewrite those which are not suitable.

1.  A father's note:
    Dear David,

    As we agreed in our conversation of May 2, 1983, you will begin cleaning your room no later than May 3, 1983. Please schedule your homework and other activities accordingly.

    Very truly yours,
    Dad

*Informal*

2.  A business report:
    Statement of Purpose:

    This is a proposal to provide the XYZ Corporation with a system for training department heads in effective written communication.

*Formal*

3.  A memo:
    July 8, 1983
    To: All The Guys
    From: Al
    Subject: Memos
    You gotta stop writing so many memos.

*Informal*

4.  A résumé statement:
    *The ability to work with people* — For a while now, I've worked with some guys in surveying.

*Informal*

5.  A term paper on computers, written for a teacher of computer education:
    What is an 8-bit microcomputer? The term *8-bit* describes the microprocessor inside the microcomputer. The microprocessor is a semiconductor integrated circuit that is the heart of any microcomputer system.

*Formal*

# ANSWERS

## FORMAL AND INFORMAL WRITING

Answers may vary, but you should note that the language used in the first letter is what makes that letter more formal: the person addressed using both first and last name; the formal reference to "your note of June 18, 1983," whereas in more casual writing the date would not be mentioned. The phrase "inquired about my health" is stiff and unfriendly, as is "please be advised," which is unnecessary even in formal business letters.

In the second letter, the phrase "thanks . . . note" is friendly and has a light tone; the phrase "yes . . . fine" is conversational, as if the writer and reader were face to face.

## PRACTICE 1

1. F
2. I
3. F
4. I
5. F

## PRACTICE 2

1. Informal
2. Incorrect (Our department hardly *ever* takes time for lunch.)
3. Incorrect (Neither Smith nor Jones *is* ready to report.)
4. Informal
5. Incorrect (Glancing down the darkened street, *we* suspected the trees were a haven for muggers.)

## PRACTICE 3

Answers to this exercise will vary.
1. This is too formal for the occasion. Here's a less formal version.
   Dear David,
       Yesterday we talked about when you would clean your room. You said that you would do it today between baseball and study time. Please do.
           Love,
           Dad
2. Just right for the purpose.
3. Too informal for the purpose. The memo sounds as if the message could be spoken rather than written, and memo is not necessary.
4. Too informal for the purpose. Here's a more suitable explanation.
       Since 1979 I've managed a surveying team of five men.
5. Just right for the purpose.

# 2.

# Determining Your Purpose

We're not use to thinking about *why* we're writing each time we pick up a pen or pencil. Yet everything we write does have a purpose. Our everyday communications are no exception. They have purposes too:

- the shopping list — to inform or remind us of what we need to buy.
- the note to the doctor's receptionist — to request insurance forms and to ask where to send those forms.
- the personal note on your Christmas card to your letter carrier — to thank him or her for special service.
- the note to a family member — to persuade him or her to make a dental appointment.

In writing these kinds of notes, we have a very clear sense of purpose. We want to give or receive information (we *inform or request*), convince someone to believe the way we do (we *persuade*), or encourage someone to take action (we *motivate*). On occasion, we want our reader to laugh (we *entertain*). Almost all writing falls under the broad purposes of informing, persuading, motivating, or entertaining.

Our more structured personal communications have clear purposes, too:

- the letter to an auto dealer — to inform the management about how poorly the car has worked since it was serviced and to motivate them to do something about it.
- the letter to fellow members of your labor union — to persuade them to vote for the political candidate who supports higher wages and better working conditions.
- the memo to the college registrar — to request a refund for the course you withdrew from last semester.

Our business communications must also have clearly stated purposes:

- the memo to all department employees — to request notice of vacation dates.

- the letter to your client — to inform him that his claim has been denied.
- the report to your supervisor — to persuade her that the facts you give favor purchasing a new word processor and to motivate her to order it immediately.

## PRACTICE 1

What are some purposes for writing memos, letters, or reports? Look at these "occasions" and identify one or more purposes: to inform, to persuade, to motivate, or to entertain. For example, consider a letter to a department store giving your new address. What is its purpose? To inform. Remember, too, that some of the examples are likely to have more than one purpose.

1. A financial report listing the company's profits and losses for the previous year.
   Purpose: _inform_

2. A letter to a client regarding his overdue bill.
   Purpose: _inform , motivate, persuade_

3. A letter to your representative telling her not to vote for the budget increase.
   Purpose: _persuade, inform, motivate_

4. A newspaper ad featuring your company's product.
   Purpose: _inform , motivate, persuade_

5. An essay on your leadership ability, written for a college application.
   Purpose: _inform , persuade, motivate_

6. A memo to your boss stating the time and place of the monthly board meeting.
   Purpose: _inform_

7. A report listing all the products sold by a competing company, plus your conclusion to increase your company's product line.
   Purpose: _inform, persuade, motivate_

8. A term paper explaining the techniques an author used to create a character.
   Purpose: _inform_

9. A memo to the office staff, assigning regular parking spaces.
   Purpose: _inform_

10. A letter explaining to a utility company why you haven't paid your bill.
    Purpose: _inform, persuade_

# Why Do You Need a Purpose?

Like most writers, you want more than to just write a better memo, letter, or report; you want to get the writing done faster and less painfully. To speed the process along, begin your writing only after you have decided on your purpose. Think about what you want the letter or memo to achieve. Establishing your purpose ahead of time will help you keep your thoughts centered on the job.

Remember your teachers' exams or essay questions? These gave you a purpose for writing.

> *Question:* In his *Origin of the Species,* Darwin used the term "natural selection." What did he mean?
> *Purpose:* To *inform* the reader of the definition of "natural selection" and give examples of it.

When you were in school, the questions you were asked served as clues to your writing purpose. Now you have to determine the purpose for yourself. And you have to put that purpose on paper and keep it in front of you as you write. Whenever you are stuck, your thoughts are wandering, or you are losing confidence, reread your purpose and move ahead.

You may be wondering how to write a purpose statement. Follow this simple formula or write your own:

> My purpose for writing this _____ (memo, letter, report, essay, etc.) to _____ (name your reader) is to _____ (inform or ask, persuade, motivate, entertain), so that my reader will _____ _____ (name the action you want the reader to take or the information or belief you want him to have).

For example:

> My purpose for writing this memo to the new supervisor is to inform her about the content of the company's safety training sessions so that she will be ready to handle her first meeting independently.

or:

> My purpose for writing this letter is to persuade my appliance customers that our new service department can handle any repairs their appliances may need so that my customers will call us before they call another repairman.

When you know *why* you're writing something — your purpose — you're more likely to organize your thoughts effectively. For example, William Howley wants a job with the Edgemont Computer Corporation. Of course, he wants the company to know about his past sales record and his awards, so they will hire him. At this point, however, Bill wants Ms. Watson to see that his sales experience qualifies him for the advertised job. That's his purpose for writing the letter. If he accomplishes his purpose, Bill will probably get the interview he's asked for.

January 12, 1985

Ms. Gail Watson
Personnel Director
Edgemont Computer Corporation
979 6th Avenue
San Diego, California 92110

Dear Ms. Watson:

My sales experiences match the qualifications stated in your January 10 advertisement for a sales manager.

Four years ago, I began selling computers for Fairchild Computer Company, and within two years opened markets in all areas of the United States. After my promotion to sales manager in 1982, my duties required me to assemble a sales team, staff new sales offices in six major cities, and track the performance of our new sales force. Other details of my education and work experience are listed in the enclosed résumé.

I'll be in San Diego the week of February 10, and would be able to meet with you any time then to answer any questions and discuss in greater detail how I could contribute to an increase in your company's sales. I will call early next week to see if we can set up an appointment.

Thank you for your consideration.

Sincerely,

William Howley

Memos, too, require a strong sense of purpose. In just a few lines, a memo must inform or request, or persuade, or motivate someone.

MEMORANDUM

TO: Martin Fletcher
FROM: Ed Wilson
DATE: 11/1/85
RE: Annual Reference Book Order

Please add the books on the attached list to your library order. Thanks.

This was a memo to inform. Notice how the memo changes when the purpose changes:

MEMORANDUM

TO: Martin Fletcher
FROM: Ed Wilson
DATE: 11/1/85
RE: Request for decision on annual reference book order

The deadline for placing the book order is November 15. Since we missed out on the early order discount last year, let's try to make up the list earlier this year. I'll approve your booklist without delay, but only if I receive it within the next week.

In this second memo, the purpose — to encourage Martin Fletcher to submit the necessary list on time — is hinted at through persuasion. There won't be delays if he gets it into Ed Wilson on time. Ed's purpose is there, though it isn't directly stated.

Reports for school seem to have the obvious purpose of telling a teacher that you've read the book or done the necessary research. Beyond that, however, your report has the purpose of informing the reader of the facts you have uncovered or the observations you have made about the book you read. Many times you will not be answering a question the teacher has posed, but rather you'll be formulating your own theory or idea, based on the purpose of informing the reader. For example, after having read Fitzgerald's *The Great Gatsby,* you have concluded that the book is not about Jay Gatsby so much as it is a story about Nick, the narrator. Your purpose is to persuade the reader that this is true, while also informing your teacher that you've read the book as assigned. Your report is likely to begin something like this:

In F. Scott Fitzgerald's novel *The Great Gatsby,* the narrator Nick Carraway is the focal point of the book. His journey from innocence to worldliness, through his acquaintances with Jay Gatsby, Daisy and Tom Buchanan, Jordan Baker, and the other characters, make this novel a story of a young man growing up in a wasteland world . . .

## Where Do You State Your Purpose?

In the example of the report, the writer has stated his main idea in the beginning paragraph. If we had included the rest of the report, you would see that he uses examples to prove the point that he states at the beginning. The reader knows what is being discussed, and the writing is clear and makes the point, whether the reader agrees or not.

In the memorandum examples, the purpose is not stated. Although in some memos you might use the RE line to state your purpose, most often the purpose of your writing remains something within you — either in your head or on a slip of paper, or on the top of your rough draft. It is important that you know what your purpose is, but you need not always tell your reader.

## PRACTICE 2

Use the following ideas to apply what you've learned about writing with a purpose. Note your purpose for writing: to inform or request, to persuade, or to motivate. Then write the letter, memo, or report as described.

1. Write a business letter to Ms. Connie Pemberton at Consolidated Savings Bank. Request the bank's patience on your overdue auto loan. Discuss why you're asking for an extension and explain how and when you'll make the payment.
   Purpose: _____

2. Write a memo to Jim Hardy, Personnel Director. Ask him to look into the company's rising absentee rate and determine its causes.
   Purpose: _____

3. Write a one-paragraph introduction for a report, "Threats to Our Water Supply," for your local environment group.
   Purpose: _____

4. Write a one-paragraph announcement to your customers stating that you are now the exclusive agents for Alphabeta Computers.
   Purpose: _____

5. Write a memo to your staff. Request that they submit a weekly sales summary instead of the usual monthly one.
   Purpose: _____

## PRACTICE 3

Read the following first sentences of paragraphs from letters, memos, and reports. Each sentence provides a clue to the purpose of the piece. Can you determine the purpose? Write your answers in the space provided.

1. (Report)   Although there are still those misinformed people who insist that alcoholism is caused by lack of

willpower, scientific research shows that alcoholism is a disease.

Purpose: _____

2. (Memo) Please send me your department's sales figures for the year-end report to the Board of Directors.

Purpose: _____

3. (Letter) I bought the washing machine marked "Large-Capacity, No. A-123," which you advertised would accommodate the clothes of a very large family; it doesn't.

Purpose: _____

4. (Report) Science fantasy, a subcategory of science fiction, bases its stories on natural laws of science, which are different from those we know to be true.

Purpose: _____

5. (Letter) We are looking for an investor who understands our industry's technology.

Purpose: _____

# ANSWERS

## PRACTICE 1

Your answers may vary.

1. To inform.
2. There are several purposes:
   a. to *inform* about the amount owed, the time overdue, and so on.
   b. to *persuade* the client that payment will protect his credit rating.
   c. to *motivate* him to pay the bill.
3. There are several purposes:
   a. to *inform* your representative of the facts.
   b. to *persuade* her that the facts require a "no" vote.
   c. to *motivate* her to vote against the increase.
4. There are several purposes:
   a. to *inform* the reader about your product (price, size, functions, etc.).
   b. to *persuade* the consumer that your product is the one to buy (it's cheaper, more efficient, etc.).
   c. to *motivate* the consumer to buy your product.
5. There are several purposes:
   a. to *inform* the reader with examples of your leadership ability.
   b. to *persuade* the reader that you are the kind of student the college would want to accept.
   c. to *motivate* the reader to accept you to the college.
6. To inform.
7. There are several purposes:
   a. to *inform* by listing all the products.
   b. to *persuade* that increasing your company's product line is the right action to take.
   c. to *motivate* management to act on your conclusion.
8. To inform.
9. To inform.
10. There are two purposes:
    a. to *inform* the company about your special problems.
    b. to *persuade* the company that the reasons you've given should prevent them from turning off service.

## PRACTICE 2

Your answers will vary.

1. Purpose: To inform and persuade

Ms. Connie Pemberton
Loan Manager
123 Main Street
Boston, MA 02864

Dear Ms. Pemberton:

You have every reason to expect prompt payment on auto loans. I regret that I have been unable to send a payment this month. I am relying on your patience and my perfect payment record prior to this month to get us through this difficult time.

For the past six months, I have been unemployed. For five of those months, I have managed to pay all my bills. However, that ended this past month.

Fortunately, I have just been rehired by my company. In order to meet all my obligations, though, I will have to send partial back payments to my creditors.

As of June 1, I will resume my auto loan payment. In addition, I will add 20% of the past-due amount. In this way, my account will be current in five months. Thank you for your patience and cooperation.

Sincerely,

2. Purpose: To inform and to request information

TO: Jim Hardy, Personnel Director
FROM: Your name, Vice-President
DATE: December 19, 1985
RE: Rising Absentee Rates

I've noticed in the past three months that our absentee rate has risen from 2.8 to 3.6 percent (using the Bureau of Labor Statistics formula). The absences are surprising, since a recent survey revealed that employees are generally content with both the working conditions and the new pay scale.

Please take the following first steps to find out why there is this increase in absenteeism.
1. Find out who — if any — are the chronic absentees.
2. Find out if there are certain departments where the absentee rate is higher than for the rest of the company.

Let's meet on February 2 to discuss what you've learned.

3. Purpose: To inform and motivate

We need water for life, yet most people take it for granted. We expect to turn on a faucet and get good-quality water because in the United States water has always been plentiful, clean, and cheap. However, too little rain in certain areas, an increased demand for water in all areas, and the new threat of pollution from toxic waste disposal make future supplies uncertain.

4. Purpose: To inform and persuade

Dear Customer:

We know you've been waiting for this good news! We are now the exclusive New England sales agents for the XYZ Computer Company. We'll be able to offer you the latest Alphabeta Computer — the one so many of our customers have wanted. Of course, we'll also stock the software and handle any servicing problems that occur.

5. Purpose To inform

TO: Staff
FROM: Your Name
DATE: 12/1
RE: Change to weekly sales summaries.

As of January 1, 1985, please submit a weekly sales summary instead of the usual monthly one. Thanks.

## PRACTICE 3

1. There are two purposes:
   a. to *inform*, giving results of scientific research.
   b. to *persuade* the reader to accept that alcoholism is a disease.
2. To inform
3. To inform the retailer about the item the customer bought and how the purchase of this item was based upon the store's inaccurate advertisement.
4. To inform the reader that one type of science fiction, science fantasy, does not base its stories on the natural laws of science as we know them.
5. To inform the reader that the writer is interested only in an investor who understands a particular industry's technology.

# 3

# Saving Time by Planning

None of us likes to waste time with preliminaries. We are eager to get words down on paper and see something tangible. For the fortunate few, forging ahead without a plan may work; but most of us need to develop some type of plan for our writing. We all know the old adages, "A stitch in time saves nine" and "haste makes waste." These sayings developed because of real-life experiences. They apply to writing, too.

## Set the Tone

Some of us only can work when surrounded by our favorite clutter; others can only work at an absolutely clean desk. Your preferred style of working is not important; preparing for it is. If you are the clean-desk type and must begin a task at 8 a.m., make certain that your desk is in order the day before.

Details that may seem unrelated to writing can cause delays if you haven't attended to them earlier. Do you have enough paper on hand? Is there a good ribbon in the typewriter? Will you need a calculator? Is the lighting sufficient?

Another aspect of planning is to let people know that you have a task with a deadline. You can request no phone calls or interruptions while you are preparing your report or special letter.

## Plan Ahead

Later in this chapter you will learn how to organize your thoughts, but planning also includes some earlier considerations. First you must have the information and tools available. After all, planning also means that when you get to the budget page of the proposal, you don't then start calling payroll to verify the amounts.

Consider these aspects of planning:

1. What facts or figures do you need to write that report, proposal, letter, or memo? Have that data compiled before you start to write.
2. Did you write a similar report or proposal last year? Use it as a model if it was well received.

3. Have you written to or received letters from the person to whom you are now writing? Have all correspondence on hand for easy reference.

4. Are you planning enclosures with your letter? Make sure the enclosures are available when you need them.

5. Does the letter require scheduling or a follow-up phone call? Have a calendar available. You don't want to say you'll call on the 10th if that's a Sunday.

6. Do you have to schedule a typist? Do you need the copy machine? Book these in advance if their availability may be a problem.

7. Are you going to ask your mother to type your term paper? Don't assume that if your report is due Thursday, you can hand it to her on Wednesday night and have it the next morning. She may have other plans.

Now that you have prepared for your writing, let's plan the actual writing.

## Develop an Outline

One of the least favorite memories you may have from school, second only to diagramming sentences, is writing outlines. Usually things would go well as far as Roman numeral III, at which point you would have an A entry but couldn't come up with a B entry if your life depended on it. Once again, we are discussing writing and — guess what? — outlining still makes sense. Don't close the book yet. Let's think it through.

An outline is simply a plan. By organizing your thoughts in an outline form, you can see clearly what direction your writing will take. The more detailed your outline, the easier your first draft will be because you will have the facts and ideas in the order in which you plan to present them.

Your outline will vary, of course, with the type of writing you are doing. You will have to tailor your outline to the task at hand. A much more structured, detailed outline would be appropriate for a term paper, while a brief, sketchy outline would be adequate for a one-page business letter. But outlining a short letter is helpful, too. By deciding the major topics you wish to cover and assembling the supporting details for each topic, right off you clarify in your mind what you plan to say and reserve the job of rewriting to tighten and sharpen your first draft.

Important! As you write an outline, don't feel compelled to put your major points in the correct order the first time — just get them down on paper as you think of them. Your mind doesn't always work linearly (in a step-by-step manner), and if you force yourself to think only in a straight line, you'll waste time. Rearrange the major thoughts in their final order after you have written them down. For example, a travel agent wanted to respond to a prospective client's request for cruise information. The agent's original thoughts tumbled onto paper in this order:

> airport departure
> ocean liner departure
> luggage requirements
> total fee
> air fees
> land fees
> ship fees
> recommended ports of call
> lines that service the recommended ports of call

In what order do you think this agent eventually placed the major ideas? After putting the outline aside for a while, he saw that, to entice the reader, the last points were where the letter should start. He organized the items, grouping them into categories and then the rest of the outline fell into place easily. When he wrote the letter, he followed his outline and writing the letter took him less time than if he had not made the outline first.

> I. Recommended ports of call
> II. Lines that service the recommended ports of call
> III. Departure details
>     A. airport departure
>     B. ocean liner departure
>     C. luggage requirements
> IV. Fees
>     A. total fee
>     B. itemized fees
>         1. air
>         2. land
>         3. ship

Have we convinced you that you should outline before you write? If you're still not sure how to do it, follow these suggestions:

1. Decide on the major topics to be covered. The scope of these topics and extent of your list will vary with the intent of your writing.
2. Review each major topic and determine the key supporting details for each.
3. Add any minor details for each key detail that you wish to include. Develop sub-groupings as you need them.

4. Arrange the major topics as they best suit your purpose. Arrange the minor topics appropriately under each major topic.

Sometimes you will have a simple outline:

I. Changes in management styles during the past decade
   A. Greater tendency toward participatory management
   B. Greater interest in workers' personal needs
II. Changes in the labor market during the past decade
   A. More women seeking more varied positions
   B. More minority access to more varied positions
   C. Better educated work force

Other times you will need a more detailed outline:

I. Changes in management styles during the past decade

   A. Greater tendency toward participatory management
      1. Companies are benefiting from participatory mangement
      2. Managers have learned that seeking staff input improves productivity
         a. People tend to prefer implementing programs they have contributed toward developing
         b. People are more productive when morale is high; staff input improves morale
   B. Greater interest in workers' personal needs
      1. Companies are benefiting from greater attention to workers' personal needs
      2. Companies have learned that the "cared for" worker is a more productive worker
         a. Many companies provide confidential, personal counseling
         b. Many companies reach out to workers' families
            (1) They provide holiday parties for families
            (2) They encourage spouses to attend company sponsored personal development programs
         c. Many companies provide in-house health services

For some people, identifying just the major topics is enough to help in writing a letter. For reports and letters longer than a page or two, you'll need to include greater detail in your outline, but that detail will simplify the actual writing.

Remember, you are outlining for yourself. This is not a document on which you will be graded, nor will you attach it to your business report. Its purpose is to help you organize your thoughts. If it were for anyone other than yourself, you would want consistency — all complete sentences or all balanced phrases. Don't agonize over form or complete sentences. Get your thoughts into the structure. If the thought comes to you in a sentence, write it as a sentence. If it comes to you in a phrase or a word, write it as a phrase or word.

The outline is not carved in stone, either. Once you complete it, review it. Is No. 1 really the first point you want to make? You can move entire sections of your outline around like pieces in a puzzle until they fit together in a way that seems best to you.

**PRACTICE 1**

Assume you are going to write one of the following pieces. Think about what you plan to say, then make up an outline for it.

1. A three-page paper discussing the effects of the women's movement on men, women, and marriage.

2. A letter to the president of an automobile corporation complaining about the many problems you have had with your car and the poor service you received from your dealer. Include a request for compensation.

3. A letter to your boss, telling him how much you have enjoyed working for him and why you must leave for another position.

# Create First, Revise Later

Okay, you tried. You wrote an outline but you hated every minute of it. You just don't work that way. You can't. You don't want to.

There is another approach, and it could work for you. You have to write a report for your boss. You have a lot of good ideas, but they are disorganized, and you don't know where to start. What do you do? Start anywhere. Just take a pen, pencil, or typewriter and begin writing down those thoughts. When you know that one idea absolutely should not follow the previous one, leave a space. Continue to put those thoughts down on paper — any way they come to you. If you prefer, use index cards. They'll be easy to shuffle around later. The important thing is to start writing.

Now, an hour later, you have seven pages of unorganized notes. Fix yourself a cup of coffee or take a short walk. Take a break.

When you've had a chance to think about other things for a while, sit down again with your outpouring. You are not going to outline, but you are going to organize. Read through those notes. At some point, you will recognize a logical beginning for your report. Put a number "1" in the margin at that point. Locate the sentence or paragraph that logically follows 1 and number that "2." Continue in this fashion.

Type up those notes in the numbered order, leaving a lot of space between sentences and in the margins. You now have your outline, or plan, or beginning, or whatever you want to call it. This plan you have written will not necessarily be a symmetrical outline, with matching or parallel thoughts and balanced lists of evidence or examples. You might have a one-sentence paragraph and then a seven-sentence paragraph. Perhaps not all of your minor points will have the evidence necessary to support them. But you've written down and organized all your major thoughts; now you can better fill in the blanks. And then you are ready to write your first draft.

## PRACTICE 2

The following notes for a letter were written by a person who chose not to outline. Apply the technique described earlier and arrange the information in a logical way. Then write the letter.

Dear Mr. Bingham:

Enjoyed meeting you at the convention. Innovative and exciting ideas. Eager to implement in our district. Presentation well planned and presented. Great deal of information. Need prospectus. Please visit. Prospectus well done. Excellent workshop. Thanks for valuable presentation.

Sincerely,

# ANSWERS

These are sample answers. Your answers will differ in content, but the style should be the same.

## PRACTICE 1

1.  The Effects of the Women's Movement on Men, Women, and Marriage
    I.   The effects on men
         A.  In the world of work
             1.  Greater competition for jobs and power
             2.  Another source of ideas and talent
         B.  In the social world
             1.  Women initiating relationships
             2.  Women's sense of identity no longer dependent on men
         C.  In day-to-day exchanges
             1.  Confusion about the rules of behavior and courtesy
             2.  Women no longer following traditional roles
                 a.  Getting coffee at the office
                 b.  Having sole responsibility for cooking and cleaning at home
    II.  The effects on women
         A.  In the world of work
             1.  Increased career opportunities
             2.  Greater respect for women's ideas
         B.  In the social world
             1.  Women less inclined to wait for a man to initiate a relationship
             2.  Women socializing more with other women
         C.  In day-to-day exchanges
             1.  Women expect men to "carry" their share of duties traditionally women's responsibilities
             2.  Women more independent in thought and action
    III. The effects on marriage
         A.  Greater sharing of responsibilities
             1.  Benefits men
             2.  Benefits women
             3.  Benefits children
         B.  More flexible role models for children
             1.  No longer clear male/female roles
             2.  Greater freedom of choice in areas ranging from careers to chores

2.  Letter of complaint about automobile performance.
    I.   I have had continual trouble since I bought this car
         A.  The high idle and stalling put me in dangerous traffic situations
         B.  The radio has never worked
    II.  The service department cannot fix my car
         A.  Repeated efforts have not corrected the fast idle
         B.  The service department does not know what to do about the radio
             1.  They claim to have repaired it
             2.  They claim to have replaced it
    III. I no longer want this car
         A.  Buy car back for original price
         B.  Exchange this car for a new one

3. Letter of resignation
   I. Enjoyed working there
      A. Freedom to implement ideas
      B. Consistent support and cooperation
  II. No opportunity for advancement
      A. Salary and position have not increased
         1. Limited funding of nonprofit organization
         2. Agency policy against hiring from within
      B. Advancement is necessary for personal growth
 III. Excellent opportunity available elsewhere
      A. Greater financial reward
      B. Faster career development
 IV. Will remain in communication
      A. To assist successor
      B. To continue friendship

## PRACTICE 2

Here's the outline.

1. Enjoyed meeting you at the convention.
2. Presentation well planned and presented, great deal of information.
3. Excellent workshop.
4. Prospectus well done.
5. Innovative and exciting ideas.
6. Please visit.
7. Thanks for valuable presentation.

Sincerely,

Here's the letter.

September 10, 1985

Mr. Roy Bingham, President
Dynamic Sales, Inc.
400 Lenox Avenue
Chicago, Illinois 60646

Dear Mr. Bingham:

I enjoyed meeting you at the National Sales Convention. Your presentation was extremely well planned and executed. My colleagues and I left with a great deal of practical information and strategies. Yours was one of the most valuable sessions I have ever attended.

The *Prospectus* you discussed clearly states your philosophy and activities, but unfortunately I did not get a copy at the convention. Would you please mail one to my office? Many of your ideas were innovative and exciting, and I am eager to begin implementing them in my district. Should you ever travel to Ohio, I would appreciate meeting with you and discussing how I have incorporated your theories into my work.

Again, thank you for a most valuable presentation.

Sincerely,
Rose Haber
Marketing Manager

# 4.

# Writing Your First Draft

---

Even the most experienced writers write a first draft. The draft gives you the opportunity to get your words on paper while your creativity is flowing, without bogging you down with the details of form and structure. Write your first draft as quickly as possible, and consider it an outline in paragraph form. You will be following your outline but fleshing it out with sentences and paragraphs.

Ploughing through a draft without pausing to sculpt the sentences might seem difficult at first. Do it anyway. You will have all of your ideas on paper, with half the battle over.

If you ever have taken a multiple-choice test, you'll remember that you were advised to answer all the easy questions first, then go back over those you skipped because they required more thought. The same is true of your first draft. Get the major ideas down on paper with as many supporting details as come easily.

Use markers to show the words and/or phrases that don't come easily. Markers are blanks, lines, or dots, and they will remind you to give special attention to those thoughts later. If you are typing the draft, double or triple space the lines. If you're writing it out in longhand, leave blank lines. This extra space will make changing and editing easier for you. If you don't have enough space on the page to make a change or improvement, you might just talk yourself out of making it.

## Be Prepared to Make Changes

Many people get "married" to the first words they put on paper. Loyalty to these words will only lead to painful separations later. Realize that although you might be very proud of your first draft, and it may be excellent, it is still a first draft. Most writing can be improved upon. If at all possible, wait a day or two before you edit or expand your draft. This lapse will give you a chance to become more objective, less tied to your first thoughts.

You say, "Who has the time for that?" But you have to include "simmering time" in your schedule even if you are a student with a term paper to write. Count on at least over night, preferably a day or two to let thoughts settle. If you say, "I don't have the time," think again. The consequences of sending a poorly written memo, letter, or report can be severe or embarrassing. If you *really* don't have the time to allow the draft to "simmer," at least put off revising until after lunch or a coffee break. Don't go directly from creating to revising to sending your communication. Leave yourself time and space to think.

## Now Let's Write

If you have followed the steps in the earlier chapters, you have focused on your purpose and developed an outline. The draft is the meat on the bones.

Suppose you must write a memo to another department head about the responsibilities your departments share. You have outlined your major issues. For example:

    I.  The functions of our departments are very similar:
        A.  We answer product complaints.
        B.  We build brand identification.
   II.  There is confusion as to clear division of duties, resulting in ineffective actions or lack of action altogether.
        A.  Clients are sometimes placed in the middle of jurisdictional disputes.
        B.  Clients are sometimes ignored, from lack of clear responsibility.
        C.  Employees appear incompetent or uninformed.
  III.  Recommendations
        A.  Develop individual departmental goals.
        B.  Hold joint meeting.
           1.  Review departmental procedures.
           2.  Set up procedures for referral.
           3.  Establish a system of checks.

Your draft might begin as follows:

The functions of departments A and X have always been interrelated. Both departments are designed to answer product complaints and build brand identification. Both departments have been staffed with workers dedicated to those purposes.

In recent years, our related goals have crossed lines and led to some confusion. Because the separate functions of our departments are unclear, we sometimes approach the same client from two directions simultaneously. Too often, as of late, a client has not been served by either department. (I) am noticing a confusion and a _____ among my staff and assume you notice the same in your department.

Notice that the draft fills in tone and detail what the outline lacked. Occasionally, for lack of the right word, a blank or marker is used. Remember, this is a draft, not a final copy. The author did not like using the personal pronoun and circled it as a reminder to rethink that sentence.

**PRACTICE 1**

Write the final paragraph for the above memo, following item III in the outline.

# More Writing Practice

Assume your topic for a report is "Everyone Must Help Maintain Our Environment." The first major statement in your outline is: "There are things each of us can do to improve our environment and to keep it healthful." How does this connect to your draft? Try this:

Few people realize the impact they, as individuals, have on the environment. Occasionally, when specific instances are called to our attention, we become aware of this connection with our environment, and we quickly and conveniently forget it again. For example, the colored dyes in paper products pollute our waterways when these paper items, such as toilet tissue, dissolve in sewer water and that water empties into rivers and streams. We can avoid this form of pollution by making a conscious effort to buy only white paper products.

Solid waste, such as bottles and cans, and the packaging that encases them, adds to a general disposal problem all communities have to deal with. We can diminish the solid waste problem on an individual basis by avoiding disposable bottles and cans. If we must buy goods in aluminum cans, we can work to establish and use a local recycling center.

Many of us adversely affect the environment without realizing it in other ways, too, such as . . . . . or when we . . . . .

The topic sentence was followed by supporting details. The writer knew more examples were needed but was uncertain as to what those examples might be. By leaving blanks, the writer can continue with more productive writing and return to this troublespot later.

**PRACTICE 2**

Following is the beginning of the next major section from the essay on the environment. See how quickly you can write a paragraph to support the topic sentence.

We can all recycle goods within our home environments.

For a clue, think about your garden, your old newspapers, your wire hangers, and so on.

## PRACTICE 3

Write a rough draft for each of the following. Remember that your draft will flow more easily if you do a fast outline first.

1. A letter to your child's teacher asking for better teacher-parent communication.
2. A memo to a co-worker asking for help in writing a report with a tight deadline.
3. The first paragraph of an essay on any one of the following topics: (a) why cats make better pets than dogs; (b) the pros and cons of allowing employers to pay teenagers less than the minimum wage; (c) the appropriate minimum drinking age.

# ANSWERS

## PRACTICE 1

To solve this problem before it reaches major proportions, I propose the following:

Each department should review the existing goals that have been set down for it and then break down those goals into individual staff operations. Let's also schedule a meeting in the near future for representatives from each department to review joint goals. At that meeting, the representatives can further clarify the differences in duties and/or exchange some duties if such action seems preferable. Moreover, the representatives will bring the results of this meeting to their departments for additional review and possible revision later. Then we can hold a final meeting to assess these reactions and finalize the breakdown of departmental operations.

## PRACTICE 2

### Choice A

We can all recycle within our home environments. If you have a garden in your backyard, you have an excellent spot to set up a compost bin, and can recycle kitchen refuse such as egg shells, coffee grounds, fruit and vegetable peels, and other organic leftovers. This compost pile will break down, and you'll soon have friable soil to use as fertilizer and mulch. Choose a spot near your garden and not far from your kitchen door. Then feed your compost pile daily with scraps, giving it a turn and a sprinkling of water and fresh soil every few days. Avoid adding any animal wastes, however, because those will attract rodents.

There could have been a lot to say about recycling in the home environment, so you might have included several suggestions in one paragraph, rather than concentrate on one suggestion, as did the writer above. If you choose to give several suggestions, however, you would need a topic sentence that summarized all those as a beginning. For example,

### Choice B

If you think creatively enough, you might soon put your local refuse collection out of business. For example, in a backyard garden, you can recycle organic leftovers by turning them into natural mulch for your flowers and vegetables. Furthermore, your dry cleaner would welcome the return of those wire hangers, to be able to use them again for your next pair of pants that are cleaned. Many towns have recyling centers for glass bottles and aluminum cans, and you can collect your empties for periodic trips to the center. Newspapers can also be collected for recycling in a neighborhood, but you can also recyle them on a personal level by using them as gift wrap, for making children's cut-outs, and as drop cloths for painting.

## PRACTICE 3

Of course, your answers will differ in content from those given. What's important is that your thoughts follow logically.

1. Letter to a child's teacher

### Choice 1

Dear Miss Jones:

Todd is not happy in school. I would like to meet with you to talk about this, so I will know how I can help him at home.

### Choice 2

Dear Miss Jones:

I am very unhappy with Todd's poor study habits. May we please meet to discuss how you and I can work together to help him? I can see you any day except Friday after 3.

### Choice 3

Dear Miss Jones:

I realize that Todd has not been a very responsible student. My goal and yours is to help him do his best in school. I think we can do this by staying in close communication. Please let me know ahead of time what his assignments will be, making certain he writes them down when given in class. If Todd falls behind in his homework, please let me know immediately. I've found that once he's missed five assignments, he becomes overwhelmed and has trouble catching up.

2. Memo to a co-worker

### Choice 1

To: John Barry
From: Maria Santiago
Re: Monthly Production Report

I just learned that I am now responsible for this report, which is due next week. Since you do such reports regularly, could we please meet as soon as possible so I can ask you some questions and establish a form?

### Choice 2

To: Sue Barton
From: Bill Martin
Re: Monthly Report

I am now working on our department's monthly report. Your recent research will be the major focus, and I would appreciate your assistance in organizing the necessary information. Unfortunately, I must complete the report by Wednesday. Please call by tomorrow so we can set a time to meet.

3. Essay paragraph

### Choice a

Why cats make better pets than dogs

Cats have a quiet dignity that dogs lack, making them better pets. When a cat wants attention, it will rub against you, nuzzle you, gently place a paw on you, and purr like a quiet engine. When a dog wants attention, it will jump all over you, lick you, or bark in a manner never thought of as quiet.

### Choice b

The pros and cons of allowing employers to pay teenagers less than the minimum wage

By allowing employers to pay teenagers less than the minimum wage, we expand the job market for teens. Employers who would not otherwise have the financial resources to hire an additional person might do so at a lower salary. Of course by opening up such lower-paying jobs, we also cut many adults out of the job market. Many employers might choose the 17-year-old over the thirty-five-year-old merely to save a few dollars a week.

**Choice c**

The appropriate minimum drinking age

Twenty-one years is an appropriate age to officially begin drinking. That minimum age totally removes liquor from the high school scene, and eliminates the problem of high school seniors buying liquor and sharing it with younger students. At age twenty-one, most people are experienced drivers, and more aware of the dangers of drunken driving.

# 5.

# Getting It Into Shape

If you've thought about what you want to write and why you are writing it, then you probably have a pretty good idea also of the overall form that your writing will take. For example, if you are writing to your representative in Congress, you'll be sending him or her a letter. If you are sending a co-worker a note, you'll want to put that information down on paper as a memorandum. If you are compiling a summary of facts and opinions for school or office, you'll be assembling a report. But each of these forms of writing has a structure of its own. Let's look at these forms, and discover how their individual structures help convey the thoughts you wish to communicate.

## Letters

When do you write a letter? Letters are written to inform, request information, persuade, thank — in general, to communicate with another person through the mail. Letters can be formal, informal, even casual, depending upon your purpose and your relationship with your correspondent.

Letters, especially business letters, should follow a generally accepted form. This form assures that the letter arrives at the proper location, gives the necessary information in a concise way, and contains your name and address so the recipient can answer your letter easily. We'll talk more about these elements one at a time, but now let's consider the basic elements of a letter.

| Introduction |
| :---: |

*Introduction.* One short paragraph states the subject or purpose of the letter.

| Body |
| :---: |

*Body.* One, two, three or more paragraphs contain the relevant details.

| Conclusion |
| --- |

*Conclusion.* One short paragraph finishes the letter with a summary, a recommendation, an instruction, or a repeated thank-you.

Figure 1 follows this format, with an introduction, further details, and a conclusion. Read the letter and notice how the opening paragraph introduces the subject, the second paragraph details the incident and provides greater explanation, and the third paragraph concludes with mention of the excellent relationship the writer has had with the company to date and with a reminder that the writer expects the reimbursement.

Although we have discussed these three major elements of a letter, there are other parts to a letter that are considered standard form. Let's look at each of these now.

## Your Address

If you are using personalized stationery, on which your name and address are printed, or if you have a business letterhead, don't retype this information (see Figure 2). If you are using blank paper for a business letter, then type your address at the top, as shown in Figure 1. When writing to a close friend or relative, your more informal letter need not include the address; see Figure 3 for an example.

## The Date

In a formal letter, spell the month out, as shown in Figure 1. Even in an informal business letter, always spell out the month, because it is clearer and in business communications dates are often very important. If you are writing to your mother in Florida, you can put the date in all numerals.

## Inside Address

For all business or formal communication you need to include the name and address of the person you are writing to because in offices the envelopes are opened by machine and mail is sorted in a mail room. If the address is only on the envelope, no one will know to whom the letter should go. The address includes the name, title or position of the person who should receive the letter, the company or organization, and the complete address of the organization.

Friendly letters often do not need the inside address because the envelope will be opened by the person you have addressed the letter to. However, if you meet

106 Goodtree Drive
Columbus, Ohio 43201
March 10, 1985

Mr. William Wellington, President
Cool-It, Inc.
738 Second Avenue
New York, New York 10017

Dear Mr. Wellington:

On February 23, 1985, while a local Cool-It, Inc., representative was servicing my air-conditioner, the tank of freon exploded in my basement. The tank was located next to my clothes dryer, thus this explosion caused damage to my dryer as well as some clothing that was in the dryer at the time. This event led to an expensive dryer service call and the need to replace a complete load of laundry. I would appreciate full reimbursement for the items listed on the attached bills.

The serviceman who repaired the dryer suggested that the malfunction was mostly caused by the freon. The spilled freon permanently froze the dryer thermostat, preventing the dryer from cooling down. A full load of towels and underwear that were in the dryer at the time became excessively dried out to the point of disintegration. In fact, when I removed the laundry from the dryer, the laundry fell apart in my hands. Prior to the explosion, the load of laundry was fine and the dryer worked perfectly.

I've always had an excellent relationship with your company and look forward to your continuing service. Your representative, by the way, was courteous and thorough in his job of repairing the air-conditioning system. I look forward to your payment within a reasonable amount of time.

Thank you.

Sincerely,

*M. Edwards*

Mary Edwards

FIGURE 1

ABC Corporation

---

231 West 53 Street, New York, New York 10022

July 10, 1985

Ms. Cary Jeffers
66 Columbus Avenue
Tarrytown, New York 10571

Dear Ms. Jeffers:

Thank you for your letter (dated June 25, 1985), asking about employment possibilities at the ABC Corporation. We receive a number of such requests each year, and must therefore limit interviews to individuals with prior work experience. Your resume indicates that you have no such prior experience, and therefore I cannot offer you any hope at this time. However, should you still want to work for our company after having gained a few years experience in the field, we would be most happy to reconsider your application.

Thank you for considering ABC Corporation. We wish you luck in securing employment very soon.

Very truly yours,

David Green
Personnel Director

DG/sl

FIGURE 2

8/4/83

Dear Ellen,

Colorado is beautiful at this time of year — at least, as much as I've seen of it. It has been raining since we arrived four days ago, but that's okay. Susan has had a chance to let her sprained ankle heal and Mickey's sore throat is almost gone.

Our evenings have been eventful. I am awakened each night at about 2 a.m. by "Lady Macbeth." Linda has been getting these horrible nosebleeds, and she wanders into my room for help. I'm sure she just has to get used to the altitude.

I understand the swimming, hiking, and shopping are marvelous here. I hope I get out of the apartment soon.

Love to everyone.

Love,

Carole

FIGURE 3

someone casually and it is likely the person does not have your address, it is thoughtful to include your address in the letter.

## *Greeting*

The rule is simple: letters begin "Dear (Name)." But the reality is more difficult. Awareness of sexism in language has led to changes in custom. A decade ago, if you were addressing an unknown person or company in general, the term you would have used was "Gentlemen." That is no longer the case. Most likely that company or department will include women. When you have an unidentified or mixed group to address, use "Ladies and Gentlemen." If addressing an unknown individual whose title you know, use a greeting such as "Dear Personnel Director." If you don't know the title, "Dear Sir/Madam" will do.

A major problem comes up when you must answer a letter from someone whose name gives no clue to the signer's gender. A letter signed by S. Thompson or Pat McEnroy will not help. In this instance, use the available information: "Dear S. Thompson" or "Dear Pat McEnroy."

If you are on a first-name basis with your business correspondent, it is appropriate to address the letter using that person's first name, as in "Dear Emily." Note that the colon is not replaced by a comma in a business letter. If your letter were a personal one — say, to your cousin about a planned Christmas party — you would address him or her with the first name and follow that name with a comma.

| Here are some standard greetings for business correspondence: | Some examples of greetings for friendly letters: |
|---|---|
| Gentlemen: | Dear Uncle Bob, |
| Dear Sir: | Dear Maria, |
| Dear Sirs: | Dearest Michael, |
| Dear Mr. Simpson: | |
| Dear Ms. Barry: | |
| Dear Dr. Moran: | |
| Dear Director of Personnel: | |
| Dear Salespeople: | |
| Ladies and Gentlemen: | |
| Dear S. Thompson: | |
| Dear Company B: | |
| Dear Emily: | |

## The Body of the Letter

Since your opening paragraph is like a first meeting with your reader, the impression you make is a lasting one. The reader expects to have your purpose revealed. Whether it is to complain, compliment, or inform, it should be clear immediately.

To clearly state the purpose and details of your message, have a plan in mind when you begin. You may need to make only a few notes, but for a longer, more complicated communication you'll want to write an outline (see Chapter 3). Write a first draft and then put it aside for a few hours. When you return, you will not only find any errors you might have made in grammar, word choice, or facts, but you will also be able to check the tone of your letter. Even a letter expressing dissatisfaction should not be nasty or rude. Remember that when your letter goes into the mail — with your signature on it — it becomes a written record of your thoughts. You will be accountable for what it says, so a second check of the facts and figures will ensure accuracy and help you avoid having to send a clarifying letter or apology.

Say what you want, clearly and concisely. Your letter may be long, but it should not ramble. Every sentence should be a necessary one. The traditional newspaper reporter questions will help you keep on track. Answer the questions who? what? when? where? and why? and you will probably give all the necessary information.

Just as your first impression is a lasting one, so is your final one. Make sure your reader knows what you expect. If you plan a follow-up phone call, say so and say when. If you want a written or telephone response, ask for it. If you began the letter by thanking the person, reinforce your appreciation in the final paragraph.

## Closings

Closings can range from "Love," to Very truly yours," depending upon the purpose of your letter. The closing should be in the same style as the greeting. A letter would not begin with "Dear Sir:" and end with "Love." Standard punctuation form requires a comma after the closing.

| Some formal closings are: | Some friendly closings are: |
| --- | --- |
| Very truly yours, | Fondly, |
| Sincerely, | Love, |
| Yours truly, | Best regards, |
|  | As ever, |

## *Name and Signature*

If your letter is business correspondence, the standard form is to follow the closing with the company name (see Figure 2), then sign the letter under the company name, with your name typed beneath the signature. If you are writing a business letter but you are doing it as a consumer (for example, if you are writing your local power company regarding a mistake on their bill), you have no company name to include. In that case, just sign your name below the closing and then type your name beneath the signature (see Figure 1).

## *A Final Reminder*

Your letter may include correct facts and well-written paragraphs, but if it doesn't look polished, your reader will be distracted from the contents. The letter should be typed neatly, properly spaced on good-quality bond paper. If it is a business letter, you should retain a carbon or xerox copy for your files. If you cannot type your letter, take pains to write neatly and to follow correct form. Personal letters, of course, may be handwritten on stationery or the paper of your choice.

Purpose plays a role in determining whether to type or handwrite a note. A handwritten thank-you note, for example, demonstrates more warmth than a typed letter.

**PRACTICE 1**

Write the following letters. Remember to follow the correct format.

1. You are Maria Borges, Finance Chairperson for the United Bank of Connecticut, which is located at 1115 Fairfield Avenue in Hartford. You are requesting information about a banking seminar scheduled in July of 1986, in Montreal, Canada. The seminar is being sponsored by the International Banking Association, which is located at 214 White Road in Montreal. The training director is Susanne Madison.

2. You are Kimberly Sumner, a teenager in Madison, Wisconsin. You live at 4 Elm Street. You have a distant relative — an aunt — who lives in New York, and has just been promoted to Department Chairperson for the Mathematics Department at New York University. Your aunt, Elsie Sumner, lives at 609 West 59th Street in New York. You are writing to introduce yourself and establish your familial connection, in the hope she can help get you admitted to the university for graduate work. You'll be in New York City next month and would like to meet with her.

# Memorandums

Letters are one form of communication — the standard form when the communications are transmitted through the mails. A memorandum is more commonly used for interoffice communications such as sharing information, setting procedures, or asking questions within a company or organization. Every business has its preferred style for memos, but the tips that follow can be applied in most situations. Treat a memo as you would any other kind of writing; that is, plan ahead and then construct clear and concise sentences that convey your intentions. Either write a brief outline or jot down phrases that will help you organize your thinking. Stick to the one subject at hand. State your purpose first, then give all the necessary facts. Tell what you want done or request information. If you are informing the reader, do so simply and clearly, keeping your tone friendly and positive. A memo need not be an edict. Simply answer the question, "What do I want to say?" Again, make sure that what you say is accurate because memos, when filed, become records.

Although a memo is very much like a letter in purpose, its structure is different. A memo usually has the following opening:

> TO: The name of the person, including his or her title and/or department
> FROM: Your name, title, and department
> DATE: The date you send the memo
> RE: The subject of the memo

A memo is not signed at the bottom the way a letter would be. Instead, the sender initials the memo next to his or her name at the top. The RE line is meant to indicate the subject matter of the memo. It should be informative, summing up the subject in a few words. For example, if the memo is to a coworker requesting reassignment of parking spaces in the company lot, the RE line would be "RE: New Company Parking Spaces."

Note the structure of the memo in Figure 4. The opening gets right to the point. Helms recalls that she and Macaulay have agreed that there is a potential problem. The memo proposes a solution. For emphasis, the solution is set off — highlighted — in its own paragraph. Other ways to visually emphasize ideas include using numbers, letters, headings, or bullets (black dots) at the left-hand margin. The final two sentences tell the reader what to do.

Note also that job titles appear next to the names. These titles can be omitted in very informal memos (see Figure 5). Other memos, which will be filed for future reference, should have the titles included.

MEMORANDUM

TO:     William Macaulay, V.P., Marketing
FROM:   Rebecca Helms, Purchasing Agent
DATE:   April 10, 1985
RE:     Purchase Agreement Number 42

When we met last Tuesday, we concurred that the above purchase agreement #42 was vague and could lead to problems once the job is completed. I propose the following change:

1.  Delete lines 4–7.
2.  Insert the following in place of lines 4–7:
    "The seller is under no obligation to accept returned merchandise 90 days after delivery."
Let me know within 2 days if you agree with this change. Thank you.

FIGURE 4

MEMO

TO:     Carol
FROM:   Sue
DATE:   May 3, 1985
RE:     1984 Dead Files

You and I are responsible for transferring last year's files to the warehouse. I'm available any morning next week. Please let me know the day and time convenient for you.

FIGURE 5

FROM THE DESK OF JOHN SMITH:

TO: Bill Greenway
DATE: December 10, 1985
RE: Monthly Report

You should be pleased to know that your December monthly report will not be due until January 7, 1986. This extension should make your vacation a little more relaxing. Enjoy the holidays.

FIGURE 6

Now read the memo in Figure 6. Does it meet all the requirements of a well-written memo? Yes. This short memo gets the job done. The subject is clearly stated in the RE line. In the first sentence, the reader learns the new due date and what has to be done. Sentences 2 and 3 show the writer's concern for Bill Greenway's well being. There is nothing wrong with a personal touch. One improvement would be to include the job titles and/or department names.

The earlier memo — Figure 5 — is a very informal one between two coworkers. No last names appear in the heading, and without these names, the memo would be almost useless as a record. Sue gets to the point immediately, however, noting co-responsibility for moving the files and letting Carol know the times during the week that she will be available. Sue then tells Carol what to do — that is, to decide on a convenient time to work together.

Sometimes you will need to write a longer memo. For example, you may want to provide background information related to the subject, as well as give current information. Read Figure 7 and note how the need dictates form. In this memo, the introduction explains the background of Dr. Taylor's idea. The first part of the memo tells what the writer intends to do. The memo then asks Martin Atkins, the reader, to do three things: read, select, and estimate. What Martin Atkins has to do is detailed as well. The memo concludes with a due date. It is effective and should result in Dr. Taylor's getting what he wants.

## MEMO

TO:     Martin Atkins, Director of Rehabilitation Services
FROM:  Bruce Taylor, M.D., Hospital Administrator
DATE:  November 10, 1984
RE:     Development of a hortitherapy program for patients

At the recent Hospital Directors' Round Table, Dr. Seymour Watson of the New England Hortitherapy Council gave a speech on the positive results achieved with hospitalized patients who had been taking care of plants. He further explained the long-term benefits of hortitherapy, especially its continued use after the patient's discharge.

Dr. Watson gave me some guidelines on raising funds for such a project. I'm going to survey the board to see how much money could be made available for our own hortitherapy program.

I've attached Dr. Watson's studies, "The Use of Hortitherapy in Geriatric Settings," "Hortitherapy in a Psychiatric Setting," and "Outpatient Programs in Hortitherapy." Please study these and decide which approach we could use at Sunnycrest.

After you decide which patients would benefit most from the program, estimate what personnel and supplies would cost for 20 patients. I'll need your cost estimates by December 16, 1984, so that I can review them before presenting my report to the Board of Directors on December 30.

## FIGURE 7

## PRACTICE 2

Select two of the following three situations below and write an appropriate memo for each.

1. From the supervisor of a department to an employee who is consistently late.

2. From a supervisor in the order department to the inventory control manager, noting a shortage in a recent shipment to a key client.

3. From a supervisor who plans to be away to an employee designated to cover that supervisor's duties during that time.

# Reports and Proposals

Letters and memorandums are very common forms of writing, but there are other instances when you will write, too. In school you may already have written book reports and themes on a variety of subjects. A report is a detailed statement of accomplishments or findings. A proposal is a request for funding to solve a recognized problem or to implement a new idea.

Since reports and proposals serve different functions, they take on different forms. Regardless of the format, however, the basics of good writing prevail. You should present your information in a clear, concise style. You need to document your facts, and if you are taking facts from another source, you must give credit to those sources. In a formal report for school, you would use footnotes. For a business report, you would include footnotes where appropriate. Your conclusions should be set off from your facts, so the reader is able to distinguish fact from opinion. In lengthier reports, it is often helpful to include a summary at the beginning so that the reader can know at the start the scope and breadth of the report without having to first read the entire report.

Most reports have a set form, similar to an outline. For example, a business report may follow this format:

| | |
|---|---|
| Cover page: | title, author, date of report |
| Summary or abstract: | a brief overview of the subject covered and conclusions drawn |
| Introduction: | a beginning section in which you set the scene, giving relevant background information and/or explaining terminology used in the report |
| Body: | the information you are sharing, which supports the conclusions you have drawn |
| Appendix: | all additional relevant data, such as sources of information, additional charts and graphs, and supporting statistics |

In preparing reports for business, check for company style by referring to previous reports. For school reports, ask your teacher what particulars are important to him or her. No one form is correct, but you should use the form preferred.

A lengthy report should have a cover page indicating the purpose of the report, the person or persons to whom it is submitted, the person or persons by whom it is submitted, and the date. The table of contents indicates the scope of the report and the organization of the body of the report. Note the cover page, table of contents, and excerpt from the introduction of a report, shown as Figure 8.

As an example of style, we have included as Figure 9 an excerpt from a report on critical thinking in education. This excerpt shows the use of a footnote, as well as a listing of points, with bullets to emphasize the listing.

REPORT*

OF THE

JOINT STATEWIDE TASK FORCE ON
PRE-COLLEGE PREPARATION

Submitted to:

Saul Cooperman
Commissioner of Education

and

T. Edward Hollander
Chancellor of Higher Education

by:

The Joint Statewide Task Force on Pre-College Preparation

December, 1983

---

*Used with permission of State of New Jersey Department of Higher Education.

FIGURE 8

## TABLE OF CONTENTS

FIGURE 8
cont.

## I. INTRODUCTION AND OVERVIEW

The problems facing our schools and colleges are many. These problems have been well documented, and recommendations for change have been developed by a multitude of committees, task forces, and special commissions both in New Jersey and across the nation.

This report focuses upon pre-college preparation in English and mathematics, only one aspect, albeit an important aspect, of a national effort to improve quality of education in this country. Our argument is based upon the assertion that the primary mission of all educational institutions is to promote learning. We recommend concrete steps that should be taken to enhance the intellectual development and academic performance of students who come to learn. We propose a plan of action that promises better education for the generations to come.

Since the mid-1970s, there has been a growing public perception that students are graduating from the nation's secondary schools lacking proficiency in English and mathematics. This perception has been reinforced by annual publication of the results of nationwide testing programs, such as the Scholastic Aptitude Tests of the College Board. Within this state, results of the New Jersey College Basic Skills Placement Test provide continuing evidence that many students entering the state's colleges are deficient in English and mathematics. Colleges and universities have found it necessary to establish remedial programs in English and mathematics; many high schools and elementary schools have shifted their focus to emphasize development of these proficiencies.

The College Board through its Educational Equality Project and systems of higher education in such states as California, Ohio, Kentucky, and Louisiana have attempted to define the skills college-bound students should be able to demonstrate in preparation for college-level course work. In spring 1982 New Jersey determined to make a similar effort. Each sector of New Jersey's higher education community developed a set of recommendations focused upon the pre-college preparation of students in English and mathematics. These sector reports became the starting point for the work of this State-wide Task Force and Pre-College Preparation.

FIGURE 8
cont.

Appointed in the spring of 1983 as a joint effort between the Departments of Education and Higher Education, the Task Force was charged by Commissioner Saul Cooperman and Chancellor T. Edward Hollander to consider the following issues:

1) college preparatory curricula in secondary schools and admission requirements in English and mathematics at the state university and at the state colleges;

2) skills proficiencies in English and mathematics that students should be able to demonstrate in order to undertake college-level coursework;

3) the relationships and distinctions between "remedial" and "baccalaureate level" work in English and mathematics, and the application of these definitions to the transfer of credits between two-year and four-year institutions; and,

4) means of using available resources more effectively to improve the pre-college preparation of students in English and mathematics in order to minimize the need for remediation in the colleges.

The scope of our report is limited, quite properly, by the charge given to the Task Force. We have concentrated primarily on the areas of English and mathematics with emphasis upon the high school level.

FIGURE 8
cont.

The Importance of Critical Thinking and Reasoning

While we focus here on specific, detailed skills, we wish to emphasize the important role of critical thinking and reasoning in the student's educational development. Although it may be more difficult to teach or to evaluate, the ability to think clearly, to understand, is an obvious necessity for quality education.

Although no exhaustive set of sub-skills cumulatively constitute proficiency in critical thinking and reasoning, there are certain identifiable abilities, including:

- the ability to identify and formulate problems, as well as the ability to propose and evaluate ways to solve them;
- The ability to recognize and use inductive and deductive reasoning, and to recognize fallacies in reasoning;
- the ability to draw reasonable conclusions from information found in various sources whether written, spoken, or displayed in tables or graphs, and to defend one's conclusions rationally;
- the ability to comprehend, develop, and use concepts and generalizations;
- the ability to distinguish between fact and opinion.*

This emphasis on the importance of critical thinking and reasoning proficiencies, however, does not mean that knowledge of facts is unnecessary or unimportant. Indeed, critical thinking and reasoning depend upon a command of factual information as well as the ability to analyze it. Thus, students should be expected both to acquire information and to use it in reasoning their way through.

---

*Educational Equality Project's "Academic Preparation for College," College Board, 1983

FIGURE 9

## Proposals

Proposals are requests for funding or for permission to implement a new idea. They follow the same general approach as a report, although most proposals have their own form. Among different companies or agencies, the requested format will vary; one typical form follows:

Abstract or summary:   a brief overview of the proposal

Statement of need:   a brief explanation of why the program or system is necessary

Goals and objectives:   detailed explanation of what will be accomplished by implementing the proposal

Implementation:   a plan for putting the program into action, including detailed information on necessary staff, materials, time, equipment, and how these will be used

Budget:   a breakdown of costs involved

Evaluation Procedure:   a summary view of the proposal and how it will be evaluated in the end

Figure 10 is an example of an abstract from a proposal. Figure 11 is a narrative of goals and objectives.

A commonly accepted form for stating objectives follows:

| Objective | Activity | Evaluation |
|---|---|---|
| 1. Students will improve basic skills. | 1.1 One-to-one instruction. | 1.1 Student improvement as measured by informal and formal assessment. |
| | 1.2 Small-group instruction in reading and math. | 1.2 Student improvement as measured by informal and formal assessment. |
| | 1.3 Development of materials to meet specific student needs. | 1.3 Student improvement through use of targeted materials. |
| 2. Students will improve self-image. | 2.1 One-to-one counseling. | 2.1 Student performance. Student responses to counselor. Student responses to formal questionnaire. |
| | 2.2 Positive reinforcement of progress. | 2.2 Student attendance. Student performance. Student responses to formal questionnaire. |

## ABSTRACT

There is a growing awareness in the field of Adult Basic Education that adults have learning disabilities that were neither diagnosed nor treated when they were younger. The general attitude in the existing corps of child-oriented Learning Disabilities Specialists is that it is too late to deal with these problems. Many adult educators are realizing that it is *never too late*.

Among the programs offered at the Union County Regional Adult Learning Center are an Adult Basic Education program and a High School Completion program. We find that the ABE students are divided into two distinct groups:

1. Those who would be able to move into HSC with time and effort, who could work on their own and in groups.

2. Those who have not mastered the most basic skills in reading or math and need and demand constant one to one attention.

This second group needs a special program of instruction and counseling geared specifically to build up skills and egos.

This proposal offers a total person package. We hope to identify specific problems, treat them as thoroughly as possible, and offer alternative solutions where necessary. We intend to help the learning disabled adult recognize his/ her disabilities as such, learn to deal with or around them effectively, improve his/her basic educational skills, his/her employability, and his/her self image.

## FIGURE 10

## II. PROJECT GOAL(S) AND OPERATIONAL OBJECTIVES

It is our belief, as well as that of our staff and colleagues throughout the state, that with proper diagnosis and individualized instruction the learning disabled, functionally illiterate adult will

a) improve his/her basic skills
b) improve his/her self image
c) become employable or capable of higher employment

Our proposed program would include testing students who give any indication at all of having a learning problem and developing a delivery system of remediation and education. While working on eliminating, minimizing, or compensating for a learning problem, the student will have a parallel program of instruction. Concurrently, we would offer developmental counseling on a group and individual basis to repair the damaged self-image of the learning disabled adult, to help him/her accept his/her condition and to aid him/her in developing an awareness of an opportunity to improve.

Learning materials will be developed in conjunction with each student's prescription. Also, existing published and teacher-made ABE materials will be used where applicable.

## FIGURE 11

# ANSWERS

Your responses will not be exactly the same as those which follow. The answer key provides samples. Do your answers offer the same facts and follow the correct form? How closely do your responses match the tone in the samples?

## PRACTICE 1

1.

United Bank of Connecticut
1115 Fairfield Avenue
Hartford, Connecticut 06120

June 2, 1985

Ms. Susanne Madison, Training Director
International Banking Association
214 White Road
Montreal, Canada M5V 2TI

Dear Ms. Madison:

   I am planning to attend the seminar your Association is sponsoring in July. Please send me program and registration information as soon as possible. Thank you for your immediate reply.

Sincerely,

Maria Borges
Finance Chairperson

2.

4 Elm Street
Madison, Wisconsin 53721
April 10, 1985

Ms. Elsie Sumner
609 West 59th Street
New York, New York 10021

Dear Elsie,

   Congratulations on your recent promotion to Department Chairperson at New York University. Our whole family in Madison is very proud of you.

   You might not remember me from the last time we met, because at that time I was only a tyke of 4 years. Since then, I've grown up and am currently enrolled at the University of Wisconsin, expecting to get my bachelor's degree next June. I'm a mathematics major, and I was hoping to apply to the graduate mathematics program at New York University. I've gotten all the application forms, but I was hoping you might be able to recommend me for admission to the program. Could we meet next month when I will be in New York? I look forward to seeing you again.

Love,
Kimberley

## PRACTICE 2

1.  TO:     John Smith
    FROM:  Manuel Garcia
    DATE:  July 9, 1985
    RE:      Consistent Tardiness

    As you know, our agency opens at 9 A.M. and clients are waiting to be served each day as the doors open. I have informed you repeatedly, in person and in memos, of my requirement that all employees be available at 8:45 A.M. You have yet to be in the office before 9:15 A.M. Should you arrive later than 8:45 A.M. on one more occasion, I will have to assume that you either cannot or will not comply with the stated starting time and I will be forced to terminate your employment.

2.  TO:     Jack Barnes, Inventory Control Manager
    FROM:  Sally Farmer, Supervisor, Order Department
    DATE:  October 10, 1985
    RE:      ORDER #67–8850/October 1, 1985

    Please note that the above order was shipped short of 50 copies of WRITING THE EASY WAY. This customer is one of our key buyers, and expects a replacement shipment within 2 days. Can you look into this and assure me that the shipment will go out immediately via Federal Express?

3.  TO:     William
    FROM:  Rita
    DATE:  February 16, 1986
    RE:      My upcoming vacation — 2/23–2/30

    Please read the attached outline of duties in its entirety before I leave on Tuesday. I will be available to answer any questions you might have regarding materials, personnel, etc. Please maintain a log of messages, and note which ones will not have been answered. John should be available to assist you when necessary. Thank you for taking on the extra load; I'll be available for same when your vacation comes along.

# 6.

# Editing and Rewriting

You've finished the first draft of your report or letter. You followed our suggestions and wrote the draft as quickly as possible. You didn't get bogged down looking for the perfect word or writing the perfect sentence or paragraph. No, you just whizzed ahead, following your plan, and left lots of room for corrections and additions. Then you put your writing aside for a day or more to become objective and develop a keener eye for errors. Now you're ready to get back to work. Get out your red pencil.

The editing and rewriting you'll do now is not the final step. It is, however, one of the most important stages in revision. Experts say that you will probably find 75 to 80 percent of your errors in this first rereading. What you don't find now is what you don't know yet . . . that's what you'll learn in Chapters 7 through 10.

## Ask Yourself

As you begin editing, ask yourself some important questions.

1.  Does your letter, memo, or report follow your original plan? If not, why not? You may have followed your plan but find that the ideas could be arranged more effectively now. Move those misplaced paragraphs or sentences. Don't hesitate to change the order, even though at the beginning it seemed the right way to arrange things. On second look, you may have found a better way of saying what you want to get across to the reader.

2.  Are your ideas well supported? If not, you may need to expand on an idea and add evidence to your argument. On the other hand, if you've gone beyond the subject matter when you've defended a point, you may need to shorten that paragraph or delete an entire section.

3.  Is the tone of your writing appropriate? Some people answer this question by reading the report or letter aloud. You can read to a friend — real or imagined — and ask yourself along the way, "Is this the way I would talk?" "Is my idea stated in a conversational way?" "Is the letter overwritten and stiff?"

Let's look at an example, written as a first draft:

Dear Mrs. Proctor:
In response to your letter of December 14, 1984, enclosed herein please find my check, dated January 1985, which I promised to send you.

At some point this writer decided that "formal" writing was better. It is not. Writing is a process of simplification, and thus you need to use simple sentences. Choose one word instead of three where possible, and avoid the trite or overused words. A simple test will tell you what to do with the sample above. If you were facing Mr. Proctor with check in hand, what would you say? Probably "Mrs. Proctor, here's the money I owe you."

That simple language would also serve in the letter. Remember Chapter I? Informal does not mean substandard, and "substandard" does not mean informal.

4.  Have you accomplished your purpose? Find a friend who is not an expert in the subject at hand. Have that person read your letter or report. If your friend is honest, you'll soon know if you've accomplished your purpose for writing.

# Check Your Language

## Wordiness

Have you avoided repeating words or thoughts? You can expect your first draft to suffer from wordiness and repetition. You could not have raced along while worrying about being original. Remember, though, that no reader wants to waste time cutting through sentences filled with repetition. When you force your reader to struggle, you try his or her patience. As you read the examples below, remember what a wise English teacher once said. After you've finished editing your work, go back and take two or three more words out of every sentence.

Here are some examples of wordiness and repetition with their corrected forms:

No:  Today in our modern world we can offer new products at competitive prices.
Yes: Today we can offer new products at competitive prices.

Note that "today" means the same as "modern world."

No: These are the basic essentials of our plan.
Yes: These are the essentials of our plan.

Note that by definition, "essentials" are basic.

## PRACTICE 1

In the following sentences, eliminate the words that aren't necessary to the meaning of the sentence.

1. Even after the machine stopped, smoke was visible to the eye.
2. We'll rent a conference room midway between our two offices.
3. If you don't understand an abbreviation, refer back to the index.
4. Rewrite the introduction again before you go on.
5. First and foremost, I want to commend your department.
6. Our study group reached a consensus of opinion.
7. Advanced planning was credited with saving the company.
8. Our product is totally unique.
9. The reason is because it would cost too much to replace the old equipment.
10. The battle produced gains that were small in size.

## Stilted Phrases

Have you avoided words that writers seem to *save* for letters, memos, and reports? Business letters are frequently filled with legal language as well as archaic words and phrases, even though they add no meaning. The example on page 58 illustrated that point: "Enclosed herein please find my check . . ." Ask yourself, "Would I use this in conversation or at any other time?" If the answer is no, strike that heavy phrase from your work.

Here are some other examples of stilted, out-of-date, and overly formal phrases that creep into business and report writing.

| Don't Use | Substitute |
| --- | --- |
| Due to the fact | Because |
| Attached herewith | Here is |
| In receipt of | Have received |
| In reference to | Concerning |
| At the present time | Now |
| Under separate cover | Separately |
| Thanking you in advance | Thank you |

## PRACTICE 2

Substitute plain English for the stilted language used in the following sentences.

1. In the process of checking your account, we have found that your bill is overdue.
2. Attached please find my check for $42.37.
3. I will take your plan under advisement.
4. We beg to advise you that our product will be on sale in May.
5. I am in receipt of your letter and its contents are noted.

## *Clichés and Pretension*

Did you use words that everyone has already used many times before? Are those words stilted and stuffy? These pretentious words are popular today, but you'll improve your writing if you choose a simpler, more precise term.

| Don't Use | Substitute |
| --- | --- |
| Utilize | Use |
| Maximize | Increase |
| Finalize | Finish |
| Prioritize | Rank |
| Optimize | Cut the cost, improve |
| Bottom line | Profit |
| Interface | Meet or work together |
| Facilitate | Help |
| Profitwise | Profit |

## PRACTICE 3

Substitute a precise word or a simpler word for the underlined word or words in each sentence.

1. We need to <u>systematize</u> our files so that we can <u>utilize</u> them easily.
2. <u>Size-wise</u>, these bookcases are a better choice for our office.
3. The way you use your time affects the <u>bottom line</u> figure for the company.
4. A larger sales force will <u>maximize</u> our profits.
5. Absenteeism <u>impacts</u> on production schedules.
6. Your report <u>legitimizes</u> our need for monthly meetings.
7. The personnel and production departments will <u>interface</u> to solve the problem.

# Spelling, Punctuation, and Grammar

Is your memo, letter, or report free of errors in punctuation, spelling, and grammar? Is the sentence structure correct? Here are samples of typical errors you might be correcting on your first revision.

1.   No:  I have skills in marketing, sales, and administration, my record of success is evident.
     Yes: I have skills in marketing, sales, and administration; my record of success is evident. *Or,* I have skills in marketing, sales, and administration. My record of success is evident.

Hint: Never separate two complete thoughts with a comma. If the ideas are related, you may use a semicolon. Otherwise, a period separates two complete thoughts.

2.   No:  My salary is $28,000, plus a substansial bonus in benefits.
     Yes: My salary is $28,000, plus a substantial bonus in benefits.

Hint: Use a dictionary to check any word you think is misspelled. If spelling is a special problem for you, plan your attack. Start by studying Chapter 12.

3.   No:  Either of these dates are acceptable.
     Yes: Either of these dates is acceptable.

Hint: When *either* is the subject, a singular verb (*is*) follows. Is this still a mystery? Take the crash course in grammar, Chapter 9.

4.   No:  Because of heavy loan losses, the bank was considering other investment opportunities or to merge.
     Yes: Because of heavy loan losses, the bank was considering other investment opportunities or a merger.

Hint: Write related ideas or a series of ideas in the same form. The word *to* is the problem here.

5.   No:  Helen Dipalmer is a better choice than me.
     Yes: Helen Dipalmer is a better choice than I.

Hint: Complete the sentence to choose the right pronoun (. . . than I *am*).

6.   No:  The Everyman Account, it is a way to use your money more efficiently.
     Yes: The Everyman Account gives you a way to use your money more efficiently.

Hint: Don't repeat the subject (The Everyman Account) by adding *it*. The word *it* is redundant.

## PRACTICE 4

Look for and correct spelling, punctuation, and grammatical errors in the following sentences.

1. When we lived in California, we fought the turnpike traffic daily, now we live in New York and can't get across town.
2. Me, I'll be in charge of assembling the graphs.
3. Neither of the authors offer a reasonable explanation.
4. Organization is a crutial step in report writing.
5. I'm sure that either the public library or the company's library have that reference book.
6. You can leave early, my schedule won't allow me to.
7. People who can make small talk, they seem to enjoy business and social advantages.
8. Heavy smoking, untreated high blood pressure, and being emotionally tense all of the time reflects an unhealthy lifestyle.
9. No one was more surprised than me.
10. The report required that I discuss the social, artistic, and what the history of the time was.

## PRACTICE 5

Read the following paragraphs from business and school communications. Find and correct the errors.

1. Foods work as a team to make the best use of nutrients, in other words, nutrients team up. For example, leafy vegetables provide Vitamin C, which helps make iron useful. Iron from peas or lentils work with protein from dairy foods to produce the hemoglobin in blood. Finally, hemoglobin carries oxygen to the cells.
2. Businessmen and Labor Leaders have alot to learn about negotiating. Some try defeating others by faking, out-maneuvering, sometimes they even lie. The new thinking, however is that negotiators from both sides should sit down together, they should deal fairly, be more open, and work toward a "win-win" solution.
3. The reasons for different people coming to the New World were different. They each had a different reason for making the trip across the sea. Some arrived to make their fortune. Some people came due to the fact that they wanted religious freedom. Others wanted land and a job.

4. My research shows that several cities in Arizona — suitable choices for our new plant site — is also saleable to our employees as an excellent place to live. In each city, transportation to the plant would be simple, direct, and it wouldn't be so costly. The weather is mild, our older employees would definitely benefit from the 76 degree average temperture and the absense of damp weather.

5. I cannot emphasize enough that developing a business plan is not simply a tecnique to keep our finance department informed. The fact is that in order to sell this company, we're going to have to show perspective buyers the direction in which we would take the company in the next 5 years. Our prospective buyer, for example, he has the right to know about our new product plans as well as our sales expectations.

# ANSWERS

## PRACTICE 1

1. Even after the machine stopped, smoke was visible.
2. We'll rent a conference room between our two offices.
3. If you don't understand an abbreviation, refer to the index.
4. Rewrite the introduction before you go on.
5. First I commend your department.
6. Our study group reached a consensus.
7. Planning was credited with saving the company.
8. Our product is unique.
9. It would cost too much to replace the old equipment.
10. The battle produced gains that were small.

## PRACTICE 2

1. Checking your account, we have found that your bill is overdue.
2. Here's my check for $42.37.
3. I will consider your plan.
4. We want you to know that our product will be on sale in May.
5. I've received your letter.

## PRACTICE 3

1. We need to <u>organize</u> our files so that we can <u>use</u> them easily.
2. These bookcases are a better <u>size</u> for our office.
3. The way you use your time affects our <u>profits</u>.
4. A larger sales force will <u>increase</u> our profits.
5. Absenteeism <u>affects</u> production schedules.
6. Your report <u>demonstrates</u> (shows) our need for monthly meetings.
7. The personnel and production departments will <u>meet</u> (<u>work together</u>) to solve the problem.

## PRACTICE 4

1. When we lived in California, we fought the turnpike traffic daily; now we live in New York and can't get across town.
2. I'll be in charge of assembling the graphs.
3. Neither of the authors offers a reasonable explanation.
4. Organization is a crucial step in report writing.
5. I'm sure either the public library or the company's library has that reference book.
6. You can leave early; my schedule won't allow me to.
7. People who can make small talk seem to enjoy business and social advantages.
8. Heavy smoking, untreated high blood pressure, and prolonged emotional tension reflect an unhealthy lifestyle.
9. No one was more surprised than I.
10. The report required that I discuss the social, artistic, and historic background of the time.

# PRACTICE 5

Answers will vary.

1.  Foods work as a team to make the best use of nutrients; in other words, nutrients team up. For example, leafy vegetables provide Vitamin C, which helps make iron useful. Iron from peas or lentils works with protein from dairy foods to produce the hemoglobin in blood. Finally, hemoglobin carries oxygen to the cells.

2.  Businessmen and labor leaders have a lot to learn about negotiating. Some try defeating others by faking, out-maneuvering, or even lying. The new thinking, however, is that negotiators from both sides should sit down together. They should deal fairly, be more open, and work toward a "win-win" solution.

3.  People made the trip to the New World for many different reasons. Some crossed the sea to make their fortune. Some people came because they wanted religious freedom. Others wanted land and a job.

4.  My research shows that several cities in Arizona, which would be suitable choices for our new plant site, are also saleable to our employees as excellent places to live. In each city, transportation to the plant would be simple, direct, and inexpensive. The weather is mild. Our older employees would definitely benefit from the 76 degree average temperature and the absence of damp weather.

5.  I cannot emphasize enough that developing a business plan is not simply a technique to keep our finance department informed. To sell this company, we're going to have to show prospective buyers the direction the company will take in the next 5 years. Our prospective buyer, for example, has the right to know about our new product plans as well as our sales expectations.

# 7.

# Writing Strong Sentences

In solving many of the word problems in your business report, letter, or term paper, you have probably made your written work a good deal more readable. Now you need to look at your sentences and make some important improvements in their style.

## Important Ideas

The sentences you write should attract your reader's interest by being *emphatic* — that is, by clearly stressing the most important idea in the sentence. You can usually achieve emphasis by placing the key idea at the end of the sentence.

Take a look, for instance, at part of a report on revitalizing city property. This section of the report emphasizes the tenants' role. The example below shows one of the sentences written in two different ways. Which sentence do you think does a better job?

> The tenant activists who conceived of the idea make the rebirth of this housing unique.
> The rebirth of this housing is unique because it was the tenant activists who conceived of the idea.

Sentence 2 gives the reader a clearer picture of the active role the tenants played in the rehabilitation project.

Look at another example from the report that points out the far-reaching results of this project.

1. The way the project was rehabilitated, particularly the reduction in the number of apartments per building, will help set the standards for future public housing.
2. The way the project was rehabilitated will help set the standard for future public housing, particularly because of the reduction in the number of apartments per building.

Which sentence leaves you with the idea that the project will have a far-reaching effect? Sentence 1 does the better job.

**PRACTICE 1**

Rewrite the following sentences. Put the more important idea at the end of each sentence.

1. Clear understanding of the company's goals is the chief aim of our new manual.
2. Investors listen when that brokerage house talks.
3. It's hard enough to prepare for today, let alone for the future, in our confusing economic climate.
4. The company could be entering a period of sustained growth if current trends continue.
5. Before supplies run out, the assistant manager should replace them.

# Unnecessary Words

You may think that there are no more unnecessary words in your report, letter, or memo. Think again. If you followed the directions in Chapter 6, you have eliminated single-word repetitions, such as "ancient, old machinery." But you can still pare away lengthy clauses and replace them with phrases or even with a single word.

No: *Because there were updrafts,* the flight was bumpy.
Yes: *Updrafts* made the flight bumpy.

No: *So that we can meet our production schedule,* we'll need new equipment by the 15th.
Yes: *To meet* our production schedule, we'll need new equipment by the 15th.

No: Order paper *that is suitable for our new word processor.*
Yes: Order *suitable* (or the *right*) paper for our new word processor.

**PRACTICE 2**

Trim away any unnecessary words in these sentences.

1. We were searching for a salesperson who had experience.
2. Here is a sample of our new design, which we have just introduced.
3. On the wall there were a great many signs that had been made by hand.
4. The farmers here raise blueberries, which are collected mainly for frozen pies.

5.  Inflation is the most serious problem that is affecting business in the United States.

# Action Words

Simplify your sentences by using an action word instead of a more roundabout group of words. In the following example, the second sentence is simpler, more effective. Notice that the verb *has decided* takes the place of a wordy verb-and-noun group.

> No:  The committee *has reached a decision* to hire you for the position.
> Yes: The committee *has decided* to hire you for the position.

Look at another example. Here again an action word replaces a verb and noun.

> No: This insurance program *makes a distinction* between new and old employees.
> Yes: This insurance program *distinguishes* between new and old employees.

**PRACTICE 3**

Simplify these sentences.

1.  The government finally made a suggestion that we delay the retirement age.
2.  You can conserve energy if you have knowledge of the sources of waste.
3.  Before you send your final recommendation, make a draft proposal.
4.  Our representative sent an invitation to their ambassador.
5.  The two countries reached an agreement to end the boycott.

# Active and Passive

Whenever you can, use active verbs instead of passive ones. Active verbs usually make the meaning more accessible because they sound immediate. They occur in a *subject–verb–object* pattern. This sentence pattern quickly answers the question "Who does what?" For example:

|  |  |  | *Direct* |
| *Subject* | *Verb* |  | *Object* |

The company offers a comprehensive medical plan.

Who? The company. Action? They offer. What? A plan. In addition, when active verbs replace passive verbs, shorter and more forceful sentences result. In many cases, using an active verb changes the subject's placement — for the better.

> Passive: The management team *was hired* by the company.
> Active: The company *hired* a management team.
>
> Passive: For novices in office management, a special seminar *is needed*.
> Active: Novices in office management *need* a special seminar.

In each case the "lost" or buried subject takes its rightful place in the sentence.

A passive verb, on the other hand, turns the thought around as in the following:

*subject*
A comprehensive medical plan *is offered* by the company.
*passive verb*

In this sentence the subject does not act; the subject is acted upon. The reader has to get to the end of the sentence to find out who did the offering.

Generally, when an active verb replaces a passive verb a more straightforward sentence results. Readers move from subject to action to object, getting the meaning as they read along the line of print. Although the passive pattern is technically correct, the more straightforward writing is the action pattern.

Does this mean that you must never use passive verbs? Not at all. Occasionally you may want to shift the emphasis of a sentence from who performed the action to who received the action. For example:

> The management team *was credited* with hiring a successful marketing manager.

In this case, the writer placed *the management team* in the subject position for emphasis. *Who* gave the team the credit is not especially important.

On other occasions, you may not want an "actor," or "doers," in the subject of your sentence. If, for example, you want to report a happening but don't want to reveal who did it, use the passive. For example:

> A work stoppage *is expected* on Tuesday.

The writer does not want to reveal (or doesn't know) who expects a work stoppage. Another example:

> A decision to close three of the five departments *was made* at the board meeting.

Again, the writer does not want to say (or doesn't know) who made the decision.

The passive sentence pattern is often used in scientific writing, because it provides the objective stance that science writers prefer. (In scientific writing, personal references, such as *I, you,* or *we,* almost never appear.) Here is how one science writer used the passive voice:

> A physical model *is* often *used* by chemists to understand the behavior of matter.

In this sentence, the subject (*model*) does not perform the action. Instead, it is acted upon (*is used*). Although the sentence mentions who performed the action — *chemists* — the writer considers the action — use of the models — more important than the "doer," or "actor."

Here are two more examples:

> A theory *is retained* only so long as it is useful to scientists.

> Some kinds of matter *are* easily *observed* by scientists.

A final note: The passive sentence pattern does have a place in nonscientific writing. However, when writers use it continually — eliminating the *actor-action* pattern from their writing, letters, memos — their reports become stilted and vague.

**PRACTICE 4**

> In the following sentences, change passive verbs to active ones. (Choosing an active verb will help you find the "lost" or buried subject. For example, in the first sentence, change "cannot be allowed" to "cannot allow." Ask yourself, "Who cannot allow?" The answer reveals the subject of the sentence.)
>
> 1. A partial credit on your order *cannot be allowed* by us.
> 2. Hundreds of these letters *are received* by people.
> 3. The material you sent us *was inspected* by us.
> 4. He *was called* a traitor by Napoleon.
> 5. It *is believed* that an additional person in the South will complete our sales group.

# Balanced Sentences

When you write, make your ideas as easy as possible for your readers to follow. One way to provide smooth sailing for your readers is to write balanced sentences. In a *balanced sentence,* a series of related actions, descriptions, or ideas are expressed in the same grammatical form. The following sentence, for example, is not balanced:

> Executives rank *business writing, office politics,* and *being delayed in airports* as their chief annoyances.

There are three items in this series: *business writing, office politics,* and *being delayed in airports.* You probably noticed, though, that the third item sounds wrong, because it's in a different form from the other two items.

The challenge is to make the third item match the first two. Change *being delayed* to a descriptive word and a noun: *airport delays.* Now the sentence is balanced:

> Executives rank *business writing, office politics,* and *airport delays* as their chief annoyances.

Here's another sentence that lacks balance:

> Robert Todd Lincoln *practiced law* in Chicago, *became president* of the Pullman Company, and *he was a director* of various banks.

Here, too, there are three items in a series. Which one is in a different form from the others? Again it is the last one: *he was a director.* To correct this error, change this word group to an action verb:

> Robert Todd Lincoln *practiced law* in Chicago, *became president* of the Pullman Company, and *directed various banks.*

## PRACTICE 5

Rewrite each sentence so that related ideas are expressed in the same form.

1. Write your evaluation truthfully and record your comments in a concise way.
2. The housing project is a benefit to the neighborhood, and it will be a credit to the sponsors.
3. The attainment of freedom and achieving national security were their goals.
4. Many people in the wealthiest nation in the world are destitute, malnourished, and don't have jobs.
5. This new machine is neither faster nor does it work more quietly.

# Related Ideas

Your sentences should be simple, correct, and natural sounding. But that doesn't mean they all have to be short. As you read the following paragraph, think about how it sounds.

> A flow chart serves as a reference document. It describes the logical flow of a program. And it's in an easy-to-follow form. Most programs will change over time. This is particularly true of business programs. Documentation is essential. The flow chart is a valuable tool.

The paragraph sounds stilted — and for good reasons. The sentences offer almost no variety. They are all around the same length (seven or eight words). Reading them is about as exciting as listening to a clock tick. Also there's no sense of what is most important or least important, because every thought receives the same emphasis. Although the individual sentences may be easy to read, they are misleading because the relationships between sentences are not explained. Only by combining ideas, by making some ideas less important and others more important, can you put some variety, interest, and focus into the paragraph.

One caution! Avoid relying on the word *and* when you combine related thoughts. *And* is useful sometimes, but it doesn't always show the precise relationship between two ideas. For example:

> A flow chart tells what must be done and a flow chart defines the order in which the steps must be performed.

The sentence gives equal emphasis to the two ideas joined by *and*. In fact, the writer meant to say something like this:

> We've already said that a flow chart tells what must be done. Now add to your information that a flow chart defines the order in which these steps must be performed.

Or, the writer might simply say:

> In *addition* to telling what must be done, a flow chart defines the order in which the steps must be performed.

Certain words and phrases help you express the relationship that sentences and sentence parts have to each other. For example, by adding the word *that,* you can establish the relationship between the first and second sentences of the paragraph.

> A flow chart serves as a reference document *that* describes the logical flow of the program.

Here's a hint. Whenever you find that you've written a sentence beginning with *it is* (or *it's*) or *there are,* see if you can establish a relationship between that sentence and the one before it.

Let's go on to the third sentence in the paragraph on page 72. The word *and* indicates that an idea in this sentence is linked to an idea in the previous sentence. Moreover, this sentence contains the word *it's*. Apply the hint given above, and your sentence becomes:

> A flow chart serves as a reference document *that* describes the logical flow of a program in an easy-to-follow form.

A similar opportunity exists in the next few sentences. You can tie together sentences 4 and 5 easily. Two words in sentence 5 — *This is* — are clues to the fact that the sentences are begging to be joined, because *this* refers to the idea expressed in sentence 4. Furthermore, *most programs* in sentence 4 and *business programs* in sentence 5 are related. Put them together:

> Most programs, particularly business programs, will change over time.
> *or*
> Most programs — particularly business programs — will change over time.

How does *Documentation is essential* relate to the previous sentences? Simple. Since programs change over time, the changes must be documented as they occur. In this case, *since* is the combining word. If you rethink your newest sentence

> Most programs, particularly business programs, will change over time.

to include the word *since*, you can include the fact that documentation is essential:

> Since most programs, particularly business programs, will change over time, documentation is essential.

As a reference document, the flow chart is a valuable tool. What word could you add to the final sentence to show its relationship to the paragraph? Try this:

> Since most programs, particularly business programs, will change over time, documentation is essential. *Consequently,* the flow chart is a valuable documentation tool.

Compare the revised paragraph with the original, choppy paragraph on page 72:

> A flow chart serves as a reference document that describes the logical flow of a program in an easy-to-follow form. Since most programs, particularly business programs, will change over time, flow charts document these changes. Consequently, the flow chart is a valuable documentation tool.

## Subordinating Words

A group of words, including *since, although,* and *if,* are especially useful in combining ideas. These words are called *subordinating words* because they show that one idea in a sentence is less important than — or subordinant to — another idea in the sentence. Moreover, subordinating words add information and lend variety to a communication as a whole. A list of some of these words follows.

after
although
as
because
if
since
though
unless
when
where
whereas

To understand how subordinating words can be used to stress one idea over another, look at the following two sentences:

We've rented all the offices. We expect the building to show a profit this year.

The writer decided to combine the two sentences to emphasize the fact that now the building would show a profit. The subordinating word *since* makes *We've rented all the offices* less important than the rest of the sentence:

*Since* we've rented all the offices, we expect the building to show a profit this year.

### PRACTICE 6

In each item below, use the information to write a sentence in which one idea is more important than the other. Use a word from the list above to subordinate one idea to the other.

1. Give me all the data by January 15. The report won't be in on time.
2. We will arrive. We expect the meeting room to be ready.
3. We requested the parts three weeks ago. The parts have not arrived yet.
4. We worked hard. Our department has succeeded.

5. He programmed the computer. He had figured out which project would suit our needs.

## Connecting Words

Another group of words play an important role in combining ideas — the *connecting words*. Two lists of connecting words follow. The first contains words that combine ideas or sentences that the writer considers to be equal in importance. The words in the second group also link equal ideas, but these coordinating words are used in pairs.

1. Words That Link Coordinate Sentences or Ideas of Equal Importance:

| | |
|---|---|
| and | accordingly |
| but | also |
| for | besides |
| nor | consequently |
| or | further, furthermore |
| so | however |
| yet | moreover |
| | then |
| | therefore |
| | thus |

2. Words Used In Pairs To Relate One Sentence Element To Another:

both — and
either — or
neither — nor
not only — but also
whether — or

The following examples show how you can use connecting words to combine sentences:

Separate: When you write an essay exam, jot down a few notes first. Use numbers to put the notes in proper sequence.

Combined: When you write an essay exam, jot down a few notes first; *then* use numbers to put the notes in proper sequence.

Separate: The police officers could not explain the cause of the accident. They could not locate a witness.

Combined: The police officers could not explain the cause of the accident, *nor* could they locate a witness.

> Separate: Several employees have expressed an interest in a company child-care center. The personnel manager will investigate the possibility.
>
> Combined: Several employees have expressed an interest in a company child-care center; *accordingly,* the personnel manager will investigate the possibility.

> Separate: Style guides discuss the steps in researching your subject. They also discuss the steps in footnoting your sources.
>
> Combined: Style guides discuss the steps *not only* in researching your subject *but also* in footnoting your sources.

(*Not only* and *but also* are both followed by prepositional phrases. When you use pairs of connecting words, be sure that they are followed by words or word groups that are alike in form.)

> Separate: The office manager filled the space with furniture that was not attractive. The furniture was not useful, either.
>
> Combined: The office manager filled the space with furniture that was *neither* attractive *nor* useful.

One caution! Avoid relying too heavily on the word *and* when you combine related thoughts. *And* is sometimes useful, but it is often overworked. More important, it doesn't always show the precise relationship between two ideas. For example:

> A flow chart specifies the steps to be taken to complete a project, *and* many business managers use it in planning their department's schedules.

The sentence gives equal emphasis to the two ideas joined by *and*. In fact, the writer meant to say that the second part of the sentence was *a result of* the first part. A connecting word like *therefore* in front of the second idea would have made the point clearer:

> A flow chart specifies the steps to be taken to complete a project; *therefore,* many business managers use it in planning their department's schedules.

Notice that a semicolon comes before a connector like *therefore, however,* or *consequently* when it takes the place of *and* in a sentence. A comma usually comes after the connecting word.

## PRACTICE 7

In each of the following items, combine the two sentences by using one of the connecting words from the list on page 75.

1. Orientation sets the stage for training. It smooths the way for what is to come.

2. Transfers require planning. So do promotions.

3. We want you to have widgets for $1.49 each. We can offer the reduced price for two weeks only.

4. We hope that the new program will attract qualified applicants from among our employees. We are publicizing it in the company newsletter.

5. The prospectus didn't say how long the project would take. It didn't include an application form.

## SUMMING IT UP

This exercise will help you review what you have learned about writing strong sentences. Rewrite the following sentences to improve their style.

1. The end of a sentence is the place where the interesting information should be.

2. Recession, high interest rates, and competing with foreign auto markets have hit manufacturers hard.

3. Once the meeting has been concluded, return to work.

4. I want to make a proposal in favor of a four-day work week.

5. The manual is printed by our Production Department.

6. Workers still expect leadership from their supervisors. And they expect them to be impartial in exercising it.

7. The supervisors thought employees had more interest in job security. Also the employees put more emphasis on satisfaction from the work itself.

8. Give the computer a program. You can instruct the computer to execute the logic over and over again.

9. Seward couldn't get congressional approval to purchase islands in the Caribbean Sea. He did get consent to buy Alaska from Russia.

10. The skeleton is a rigid or semirigid structure that is a support for animals' soft tissues. It provides leverage for muscular action.

# ANSWERS

## PRACTICE 1

1. The main effect of our new manual is a clear understanding of the company's goals.
2. When that brokerage house talks, investors listen.
3. In our confusing economic climate, it's hard enough to prepare for today, let alone for the future.
4. If current trends continue, the company could be entering a period of sustained growth.
5. The assistant manager should replace supplies before they run out.

## PRACTICE 2

1. We were searching for an experienced salesperson.
2. Here is a sample of our newly introduced design.
3. On the wall there were a great many handmade signs.
4. The farmers here raise blueberries mainly for frozen pies.
5. Inflation is the most serious problem affecting business in the United States.

## PRACTICE 3

1. The government finally suggested that we delay the retirement age.
2. You can conserve energy if you know the sources of waste.
3. Before you send your final recommendation, draft a proposal.
4. Our representative invited their ambassador.
5. The two countries agreed to end the boycott.

## PRACTICE 4

1. We cannot allow a partial credit on your order.
2. People receive hundreds of these letters.
3. We inspected the material you sent us.
4. Napoleon called him a traitor.
5. We believe that an additional person in the South will complete our sales group.

## PRACTICE 5

1. Write your evaluation truthfully and record your comments *concisely*.
2. The housing project is a benefit to the neighborhood and a *credit to the sponsors*.
3. *Attaining* freedom and achieving national security were their goals.
   *or*
   The attainment of freedom and the achievement of national security were their goals.
4. Many people in the wealthiest nation in the world are destitute, malnourished, and *jobless*.
5. This new machine is neither faster nor *quieter*.

## PRACTICE 6

1. Unless you give me all the data by January 15, the report won't be in on time.
2. When we arrive, we expect the meeting room to be ready.
3. Although we requested the parts three weeks ago, they have not arrived yet.
4. Because we worked hard, our department has succeeded.
5. He programmed the computer after he had figured out which project would suit our needs.

## PRACTICE 7

1. Orientation not only sets the stage for training but also smooths the way for what is to come.
2. Both transfers and promotions require planning.
3. We want you to have the widgets for $1.49 each; however, we can offer this reduced price for two weeks only.
4. We hope that the new program will attract qualified applicants from among our employees; therefore (*or* consequently *or* accordingly), we are publicizing it in the company newsletter.
5. The prospectus didn't say how long the project would take, nor did it include an application form.

## SUMMING IT UP

1. The interesting information should be at the end of a sentence.
2. Recession, high interest rates, and competition with foreign auto markets have hit manufacturers hard.
3. After the meeting, return to work.
4. I propose a four-day work week.
5. Our Production Department prints the manual.
6. While workers still expect leadership from their supervisors, they expect them to be impartial in exercising it.
7. Although the supervisors thought employees were more interested in job security, the employees put more emphasis on job satisfaction.
8. After you program a computer, you can instruct it to execute the logic over and over again.
9. Although Seward couldn't get congressional approval to purchase islands in the Caribbean Sea, he did get consent to buy Alaska from Russia.
10. The skeleton is a rigid or semirigid structure supporting animals' soft tissues and providing leverage for muscular action.

# 8.

# Developing Powerful Paragraphs

A *paragraph* is a group of sentences about one topic. The first line of each new paragraph is usually indented about an inch, to let the reader know that a new topic is about to be discussed.

What is the importance of this information to you as a writer? The answer is clear: in every paragraph you write, develop one idea fully, and don't wander from that topic to another one. It's unfair to your readers, for instance, to start a paragraph with *fossils* as your topic and then to finish with *volcanic eruptions* as the central thought.

As you read the following paragraph, think about the one idea that the writer develops. What is that idea?

> Research shows that habits and lifestyle in the 1980's are a greater risk to our health than any other factor. Where pneumonia and diphtheria took their toll in the nineteenth century, smoking, poor diet, and drinking exact their toll in the twentieth. These poor habits greatly increase our chances of developing cancer and heart disease, or of dying in an auto accident.

Explanation: The writer states the topic in the first sentence: our habits and lifestyle, not other factors, put our health at risk. The rest of the paragraph supports that statement. The paragraph explains what some of the risks used to be (pneumonia and diphtheria) and what they are now (smoking, poor diet, drinking). The last sentence tells what lifethreatening results our habits can lead to.

It's clear, then, that each paragraph must have a topic. Writing experts disagree, though, on the appropriate length for a paragraph. Some writers say that a paragraph should be at least five sentences long. Others suggest that the length depends on the topic. Experts in business writing note that while the topic should be expressed clearly, the paragraph shouldn't be overloaded. People in business want to be able to get the writer's message quickly, without having to plow through a lengthy explanation.

## PRACTICE 1

Read these paragraphs. In each case the writer develops one idea. State that idea in your own words.

1. Computers have not only changed how fighters fly, they have also changed the demand of men who will be flying them. In the past, pilots had to be taught the system. Now many trained technicians or systems operators also know how to fly. This is not to say that bespectacled prodigies, weighing 95 pounds and carrying texts on advanced computer technology in one hand and Dramamine in the other, are about to start coming out of fighter pilot school. As long as pilots are needed in fighters — which may not be much longer — the emphasis will be on physically fit individuals with excellent sight and very sound reflexes. But from now on, fighter pilots will also tend to have engineering and technical backgrounds.

Topic: _____

2. Our business plan should answer two important questions: how is our business doing right now, and where do we want the business to be in five years' time? To write the plan, we'll have to take a careful look at such factors as our current products, our financial needs and resources, and our management policies. A critical look at the company's strengths and weaknesses will enable us to develop strategies to reach our long-term goals.

Topic: _____

# The Topic Sentence

A sentence that presents the topic is called the *topic sentence*. Topic sentences are often at the beginning of the paragraph. There are several good reasons for that placement. First, it's the easiest way for the writer to develop the topic. Second, it gives the reader the most important idea immediately. Placed first, it prepares the reader for what is to come. In business writing, this approach is particularly useful, because executives and others often want to skim through a paragraph to get the main idea quickly. For example, read the following paragraph.

Community leaders can take an active part in slowing down demand for water and seeing that it is not poisoned. To begin, leaders can set up conservation programs to educate the public. They can enact measures to conserve water in public schools, hospitals, and other buildings. In addition, they can change the pricing system to discourage high-volume water use, as well as identify the high-water users in industry and help them develop conservation plans. Finally, community leaders can try to convince people and industry not to poison the water we have left.

Were you able to locate the topic sentence in the paragraph above? Underline it and notice where it is in the paragraph.

The topic doesn't have to be stated in the first sentence, however. Sometimes the topic sentence is more effective later in the paragraph. If the topic sentence appears in the middle of the paragraph, for instance, the writer can use the opening sentence as a transition from the previous paragraph. If a topic sentence comes at the end, the paragraph builds to a climax, holding the reader's interest until the last sentence. Experienced writers know that if every paragraph begins with the topic sentence, they have to work very hard to maintain the reader's interest. The best advice is to vary your approach, with topic sentences appearing first, in the middle, and last.

## PRACTICE 2

Underline the topic sentence in each paragraph.

### I

Reproduction, of course, is the key to an organism's survival. Failure to reproduce means no progeny. If this continues, it means an end to the species. And offspring must be produced in sufficient numbers so that some few will survive all threats of their environment. So salmon must lay 28 million eggs in one season while oysters must produce four times that amount to survive their predators and other risks and maintain their species in the world.

### II

But installing telephone service for anyone who wants it is no longer our only interest. The newest developments in telecommunications — including information sharing — offer more exciting possibilities. We predict that our company will soon be able to link up your home or office with the worldwide information explosion.

III

Now that you've determined your purpose for writing, and know who your reader will be, you're ready to write some research notes. Used in the following way, a card system will keep your notes organized and prevent your retracing steps. Use at least two cards for each publication. Use the first card to record the title, author, publisher, page number, catalog number, and date of publication for each book or periodical. Be sure to give each card a cross-reference number. Then, on your second (third, fourth, etc.) card, along with your research, write the cross-reference number from your title card.

## Purpose: First, Last, and Always

Just when you thought you'd never hear it again, here's another reminder: purpose is everything — or nearly everything. As we said in Chapter 2, when you know *why* you're writing something — to inform, or to persuade, or to motivate to action — you're more likely to organize your thoughts effectively. When you're editing your work, ask yourself, "How does this paragraph fit in with the purpose of my report, letter, or memo?" That's what each paragraph should do. Furthermore, every paragraph has the characteristics of a report as a whole: a purpose, a topic, and supporting ideas that carry out the topic. Here's a paragraph from a health report whose main purpose is to inform the reader about the dangerous effects of the sun's ultraviolet rays.

Keep three questions in mind as you read the paragraph. 1. What is the purpose of the paragraph? (Persuade? Inform? Motivate?) 2. Do you think this paragraph advances the purpose of the report? Explain. 3. Which sentence states the topic?

> Ultraviolet radiation from the sun can reach you and burn your skin even if you're not directly in the sunlight. If you love to sunbathe, you should know that 80 percent of ultraviolet radiation can get through a layer of clouds. A beach umbrella will only partially protect you, because ultraviolet rays reflect off the sand. Even light beach clothing allows 25 percent of the ultraviolet rays to reach your skin. Don't count on a swim to shield you either, since 50 percent of the sun's ultraviolet radiation will reach those parts of your body that are under water.

Let's answer the three questions stated above. The purpose of the paragraph is to inform. The paragraph ties directly into the overall purpose of the report because readers need to know how ultraviolet radiation reaches them in order to avoid the dangerous rays. The paragraph gives information that dispels myths about protection under the sun. Finally the writer gets right to the point by placing the topic in the first sentence.

# What's Your Plan?

Paragraphs don't just happen. Writing each paragraph calls for some careful preparation on your part. The first step is to identify your topic and then state it in a topic sentence. The next step is to select details to support, or back up, the topic so that your paragraph will be adequately developed and unified. A *well-developed paragraph* provides enough information to explain the topic in a meaningful way: it doesn't leave the reader hanging in midair, unsure of the point the writer is making. In a *unified paragraph,* every idea presented is directly related to the topic sentence.

As you draft your topic sentence, keep in mind the *plan of development* that you will be using when you write the paragraph. The way you word your topic sentence and the type of details you include in the paragraph will depend on the plan you have chosen. Sticking to this plan will make it easier for you to develop your ideas and will help keep the paragraph unified.

There are a number of different plans that writers use:

- Give examples that explain the topic sentence.
- Defend the opinion stated in the topic sentence.
- Compare and contrast two items stated in the topic sentence.
- Describe chronologically, or in time order, what the topic sentence states.
- Define a word or explain a process stated in the topic sentence.
- Link the topic sentence to an earlier topic or one to come.

Following are examples of different kinds of paragraph development. Before you read the explanation that follows each paragraph, decide what you think the writer's plan was. Use the list above to name each plan.

1. A substance grown from molds ushered in the age of antibiotics. An English bacteriologist, Alexander Fleming, discovered penicillin in 1928 when some mold he was growing fell from a culture plate. Fleming noticed that the mold had destroyed the bacteria around it. Following up on his accidental discovery, Fleming grew the mold on broth. Then he placed drops of the broth into test tubes containing disease-carrying bacteria. The broth stopped the bacteria's growth. Fleming called the broth penicillin. Later, the term was applied only

to the active chemical substance formed in the broth. In 1940, two other scientists, Howard W. Florey and Ernst Chain, discovered how penicillin could be purified for use.

Plan _____

Paragraph 1 is developed chronologically; that is, events are described in the order in which they took place. Two dates stand out: 1928 in the second and 1940 in the last sentence. Indeed, the paragraph records the history of penicillin, beginning with the discovery of some mold that had accidentally fallen from a culture plate. The paragraph also contains several words that act as clues to the chronological pattern. *Following, then,* and *later* all move the paragraph along in a time sequence.

2. We prefer technical schools that accept students from a variety of backgrounds. The school should welcome high school juniors and seniors who are prepared to tackle both the academic and the technical courses. High school graduates who choose vocational training instead of college would also benefit from the technical school's curriculum. And possibly the most important program in the school would be for men and women in their early twenties who have had low-paying jobs and are ready to come back to school to learn a trade.

Plan _____

In Paragraph 2, the writer states a preference in the topic sentence: We prefer technical schools that accept students from a variety of backgrounds. Each sentence that follows describes one of those backgrounds. Sentences two, three, and four offer *examples that support the topic sentence.*

3. The characteristics that help a plant survive in a particular environment are called *adaptations.* For example, only certain plants can adapt to the desert environment. The barrow cactus' structure allows it to gather water through its widespread root system after an infrequent rainstorm. Furthermore, the cactus' fleshy stem is well adapted to store a large amount of water.

Plan _____

In Paragraph 3, the topic sentence *defines* the term *adaptations*; the remaining sentences describe *adaptation* in a particular type of plant.

Now try your hand at identifying paragraph plans in the following practice exercise.

## PRACTICE 3

Label each paragraph according to its plan. Use the list on page 84 to name each plan.

1. While discount telephone services can reduce a company's long-distance telephone expenses, they do not take into account two important factors. First, telephone companies throughout the country have been converting to message unit billing, which means that local calls will no longer be "free" and will instead be billed as toll charges according to the length of conversation. As message unit billing expands nationwide, more and more telephone users will begin to feel the heavy burden of local toll charges, charges that cannot be reduced with discount telephone service carriers. Second, since they cannot change the habits of telephone users, discount communications services by themselves are not totally effective in reducing toll charges. People are not generally prudent in the way they use the telephone. This is particularly true in business, where company phones are often used for personal calls and where business-related calls are overextended.

2. In my opinion, book censorship is a foolish and wasteful practice. Students can easily find these forbidden books elsewhere. Yet, we deprive readers of adequate teaching that would enlarge their thinking about the controversial contents of these books. We forget that qualified teachers not only instruct about literary styles, but also present the social attitudes of the times together with the author's intent, allowing the student to understand the book's controversial nature.

3. While reading Thomas Mann's "Tonio Kröger" and Franz Kafka's "The Judgement," one immediately notices contrasts in the authors' styles. Mann displays a highly detailed and descriptive style. His characters as well as their ideas are intricately drawn. Mann presents a full story, one that covers much of a lifetime, with an established plot that conveys a theme. On the other hand, Kafka develops his characters

vaguely; his descriptions and statements frequently negate each other. Furthermore, this author presents more of a day-in-the-life story, in which little background is given. Ultimately, Kafka leaves the meaning of the story open to the reader's interpretation.

4.  After World War II, Jacques-Yves Cousteau's attention turned to research on devices for underwater exploration. In 1943, with Emile Gagman, Cousteau received great acclaim for his invention of an underwater breathing apparatus, the Aqualung. The Aqualung, which allows divers to spend prolonged periods of time underwater, is used widely in exploration, in salvage operations, in nautical archaeology, as well as in recreational diving. Later, in 1959, with Jean Mollard, Cousteau invented the Diving Saucer, a highly maneuverable submarine in which several observers can film the ocean's depth. Finally, in the early 1980s, Cousteau (along with his research team) added the Maulian Vent, a wind-powered ship with no sails, to his credits.

5.  In this chapter, we will follow, step by step, the process of developing a solution to a problem suitable for submitting to a computer. The problem we've chosen is very general: computing an average. We'll begin by carefully defining the problem to be solved. Next, we'll structure a human-level solution, using such generally accepted and understood everyday tools as a pocket calculator and a counter. Having specified a fairly complete human-level solution, we'll briefly discuss a few elementary computer concepts and restructure our solution to fit the requirements of these machines, developing a flow chart and the description of the data to be processed. Once we've completed these tasks, we'll be ready to begin coding the program in BASIC.

6.  On the other hand, this same technology that provides an information and entertainment boon to the home viewer, presents an ongoing problem for the producers and copyright owners. Questions arise. How will copyright owners be reimbursed for providing free programs? Is our existing copyright law obsolete since the private viewer has the ability to take information that was meant to be shown only once? The old solutions to copyright infringement don't seem to apply.

# Pulling It Together

A paragraph that is *planned* — that presents only one topic and then provides details to support that topic — is on the right track. Still, it may not be the best it can be. Transition, or pointer words, can make a paragraph more interesting and certainly clearer. *Transition words or phrases* tie the sentences together and help the reader follow the writer's line of thought.

Here's a paragraph with transition words in italics. What do the words do for you, the reader?

> Dear Mr. Gordon:
>
> We know from your initial report that there is a strong market for widgets in the Northeast. *Now* the CEO and I would like you to begin a feasibility study. *In fact,* we will wait for the study before we talk to our banks about possible loans. *Moreover,* since manufacturing this new product would require additional staff, we'll need as much as six months to interview and hire candidates.

As you can see, transition words are not merely thrown into a paragraph. They're placed where they can contribute to the paragraph's meaning, and smooth the reader's way from the beginning of the paragraph to the end. In this paragraph, the word *now* switches the reader from the past (the initial report) to the present (the feasibility study). Then the words *in fact* emphasize that until Mr. Gordon does his job, the company cannot proceed with its plans. Finally, the word *moreover* introduces another reason why the company cannot begin manufacturing widgets for some time.

The more you read — both fiction and nonfiction — the more you'll realize that transition words fall into categories:

| | |
|---|---|
| Time: | *now, then, first, second, finally, meanwhile* |
| Emphasis: | *indeed, in fact, certainly, clearly* |
| Contrast: | *yet, however, but, although, nonetheless, on the contrary, on the other hand, nevertheless* |
| Similarity: | *similarly, just as, likewise* |
| Illustration: | *for example, for instance, to illustrate, in this way* |
| Conclusion: | *therefore, consequently, in other words, in conclusion* |
| Addition: | *moreover, in addition* |

## PRACTICE 4

1. Insert the words *nonetheless, indeed* and *meanwhile* where they belong in the following paragraph:

Dear Ms. Harris:

Please forgive us: We've just discovered that our computer has been spewing out duplicate bills. _____
We've found that you paid your bill within ten days of receiving it. We hope, _____, that you will remain a friend. _____
_____ you are a valued customer.

2.  Insert the words *on the contrary* and *furthermore* where they belong in the following paragraph:

I really don't think it is fair to blame this decline of eloquence entirely on the general public. As the entertainment industry has grown into its presently mammoth proportions, the distractions available to the common man, from movies to music to the opera, have quietly pushed ceremonial orations, political debates, and general knowledge lectures off the podium. Instead of using this mass communication marvel to make important statements, the "minds" of Hollywood produce "mindless rot" which the masses kindly consume and then ask for more.

3.  Insert the words *finally, first,* and *then* where they belong in the following paragraph:

In his *Book of Lists,* Irving Wallace ranks fear of public speaking among the top ten fears, right after death by violence. You can beat that fear by being well prepared and by following this plan in your next presentation. Capture your audience's attention immediately with a question or a statement that pulls the listeners out of their own thoughts and onto your wavelength. State your position. Give your listeners a way to think, a viewpoint. Follow up with statistical charts, ideas in picture form, or visual aids which tell your story. If you want your listeners to do something, leave them with something to do: a sample letter to their state representatives (with addresses), a ready-to-mail order form, a request for information to your company.

# ANSWERS

## PRACTICE 1

1. Computers have changed how fighter planes fly; they've also changed the demands we make on pilots.
2. Writing a business plan will help the company examine its present status and its plans for the future.

## PRACTICE 2

1. Reproduction, of course, is the key to an organism's survival.
2. We predict that our company will soon be able to link up your home or office with the worldwide information explosion.
3. Used in the following way, a card system will keep your notes organized and prevent your retracing steps.

## PRACTICE 3

1. Plan: Gives examples that explain the topic sentence.
2. Plan: Defends the opinion stated in the topic sentence.
3. Plan: Gives examples that contrast the work of the two authors.
4. Plan: Describes chronologically what the topic sentence states.
5. Plan: Defines (or explains) a process.
6. Plan: Links the topic sentence to an earlier topic.

## PRACTICE 4

1. Dear Ms. Harris:
   Please forgive us! We've just discovered that our computer has been spewing out duplicate bills. *Meanwhile*, we've found that you paid your bill within ten days of receiving it. We hope, *nonetheless*, that you will remain a friend. *Indeed*, you are a valued customer.
2. I really don't think it is fair to blame this decline of eloquence entirely on the general public. *On the contrary*, as the entertainment industry has grown into its presently mammoth proportions, the distractions available to the common man from movies to music to the opera have quietly pushed ceremonial orations, political debates, and general knowledge lectures off the podium. *Furthermore*, instead of using this mass communication marvel to make important statements, the "minds" of Hollywood produce "mindless rot" which the masses kindly consume and then ask for more.
3. In his *Book of Lists*, Irving Wallace ranks fear of public speaking among the top ten fears, right after death by violence. You can beat that fear by being well prepared and by following this plan in your next presentation. *First*, capture your audience's attention immediately with a question or statement that pulls the listeners out of their own thoughts and onto your wavelength. *Then*, state your position. Give your listeners a way to think, a viewpoint. Follow up with statistical charts, ideas in picture form, or visual aids which tell your story. *Finally*, if you want your listeners to do something, leave them with something to do: a sample letter to their state representatives (with addresses), a ready-to-mail order form, a request for information to your company.

# 9.

# Surviving Grammar

---

Eliza Doolittle was "labeled" by her Cockney accent. Often avoidable errors in grammar can destroy one's image. Sometimes, because "everyone" misuses a word or phrase, we assume the misuse is acceptable. It may be okay between friends in conversation, but not on paper, in school, or the office. Following is an awareness test. The paragraph includes several commonly accepted errors. Can you spot them? Can you correct them?

> Everyone, in their own way, make the best of a difficult situation. For example, my boss and me were having lunch at a popular restaurant. Suddenly, a person who neither of us knew came to our table. He pretended that he knew my boss and I very well and asked to join us for lunch. We tried to say no, but he sat right down. As things turned out, he was very interesting company. We had to leave suddenly. The reason was because we had a meeting. We thanked him for lunch and left.

Did you find the errors? Read the corrected paragraph.

> Everyone, in <u>his</u> own way, <u>makes</u> the best of a difficult situation. For example, my boss and <u>I</u> were having lunch at a popular restaurant. Suddenly, a person <u>whom</u> neither of us knew came to our table. He pretended that he knew my boss and <u>me</u> very well and asked to join us for lunch. We tried to say no, but he sat right down. As things turned out, he was very interesting company. We had to leave <u>suddenly because</u> we had a meeting. We thanked him for lunch and left.

Lack of agreement of subject and verb and misuse of pronouns are two common errors.

# Agreement Between Subject and Verb

Do you remember the two basic sentence patterns you read about in Chapter 7?

*Action*            *Direct*

*Subject*   *Word*        *Object*

The company offers a comprehensive medical plan.

And

*Word or words*
*that complete*
*the verb portion*
*Subject*        *of the sentence*

A medical plan is offered by the company.

*Passive*
*Verb*

You have to know about sentence patterns, subjects, and verbs, to understand agreement of subject and verb. In each of the example sentences above, the subject is singular — one company, one plan. Each singular subject is followed by a singular verb — *offers* and *is*. How do you know which verb form to use? Follow these steps to ensure agreement.

1. Decide if the subject is singular or plural. For example, *John (use/uses) the program to edit his reports.*
2. If the subject is third person (he, she, it, or a *name*) singular, as this is, add an *s* to the end of the verb. This may seem contradictory because at other times an *s* means plural (on subject words or nouns). This is not the case with verbs. Added as a verb ending, the *s* means the verb is singular. For example, *John* (singular subject) *uses* (singular action verb) *that program to edit his report.*
3. If the subject is plural, use the verb in its base form. For example, *Our employees* (plural subject) *use* (plural action verb — no *s*) *that program to edit their reports.*

For a first or second person subject, singular or plural, the *s* is not added to the verb:

| | |
|---|---|
| I use | we use |
| you use | you use |
| he, she, it uses | they use |

4. Check any pronoun that refers to the subject. It, too, must agree with the subject in number. For example, *John uses that program to edit his reports.* Or, *Our employees used that program to edit their reports. His,* a singular pronoun, refers to *John,* a singular subject. *Their,* a plural pronoun, refers to *employees,* the plural subject.

Words such as *everyone, each, any, everybody, somebody,* and *anybody* are *singular. None* and *some* can be used both in the singular and in the plural. For example:

> I know *each* of you enjoys studying on our campus.
> *Somebody* interrupt*s* whenever I speak.
>
> *None* of our staff *leaves* before 6 P.M.
> *None* of the meeting times *is* acceptable.
> *Some* of the housing *is* ready.
> *Some* of the houses *are* ready.

## For Special Handling

Review the forms of the verb *to be.*

The verb *to be* often confuses people. Note the chart below. These are the correct uses of the present tense forms of to be. Note that "you is" is never correct. Whether *you* refers to one person or twelve, "you are" is the correct form. Note, too, that "they are" is correct. "They is" is never acceptable.

| Singular | Plural |
|---|---|
| I am | we are |
| you are | you are |
| he, she, it is | they are |

These are the past tense forms of the verb *to be:*

| | |
|---|---|
| I was | we were |
| you were | you were |
| he, she, it was | they were |

Note that *was* is correct only when used with *I, he, she, it* (or a name for the singular person).

The same rule applies to the verb *to have*. Note when *has* is used:

| | |
|---|---|
| I have | we have |
| you have | you have |
| he, she, it has | they have |

The past tense is easier. Everyone *had*.

| | |
|---|---|
| I had | we had |
| you had | you had |
| he, she, it had | they had |

Many problems of agreement between subject and verb occur when the verb does not directly follow the subject in the sentence.

There is no question that the following sentence is correct:

The applications arrive in the morning mail.

*Applications* is plural and *arrive* (without an "s") is the plural verb form. The next sentence is clearly correct, too:

All of the applications arrive in the morning mail.

*All* is the subject of that sentence, not *applications*. If, however, we quickly read "applications arrive," as the subject and verb, we won't get into trouble. *All* is plural, too. Please note the following description:

   S       modifier     V
All of the applications arrive in the morning mail.

Note the following sentence:

One of the applications arrive in the morning mail.

By quickly misinterpreting "applications" as the subject, you can miss the error in the sentence.

What is the subject? *One. One arrives.*

   S               V
One of the applications arrives in the morning mail.

## PRACTICE 1

Complete the following paragraph, selecting the correct verb form to complete each blank.

The subway platform is very crowded at 8 a.m. Tourists (*rush, rushes*) to get started early. Many of the businessmen and women (*attempt, attempts*) to get to their offices before 9 a.m., and workers returning from the 12 a.m. shift also (*crowd, crowds*) the platform. One of the conductors (*is, are*) especially interesting to watch during this hectic time. He (*shout, shouts*) directions and (*signal, signals*) with his hands as though he were a performer in a Broadway show. Crowds of people (*stop, stops*) in their haste to observe this showman. One of the commuters (*offer, offers*) coffee to him each morning. Without skipping a beat, he (*accept, accepts*) it with a wink of thanks.

## For Special Handling

Words such as *all, few, several, both,* and *many* are plural.

> Both of my brief cases *are* ruined.
> Many of the dishes in this restaurant *are* spicy.
> Several performers *host* parties after the show.
> A few of the instructors *have* additional jobs.
> All of the applicants *were* interviewed last Friday.

## For Special Handling

*Either . . . or* takes a verb that agrees with the *second* choice.

> Either the tree or the bushes *have* to go.
> Either the bookkeepers or the accountant *mails* the statement.
> Either of those desks *is* fine.

The last example is tricky. In this case, *either* means "either one." The phrase "of those desks" describes, or modifies, *either*, which is the subject of the sentence.

### PRACTICE 2

Select the correct word or words to complete each sentence.

1. Everyone (*work, works*) at (*their, his/her*) own pace.
2. Any of these dresses (*is, are*) suitable for that occasion.
3. John and he often (*go, goes*) to Tilli's for lunch.
4. Few men (*has, have*) done this job as well as Martin.
5. Either of those courses (*meet, meets*) the requirement.
6. Either Arnold or John (*own, owns*) that Honda.
7. Several of the office clerks (*know, knows*) how to access the computer.
8. None of those posters (*belong, belongs*) in this room.

9. Either Felice or her cousins (*babysit, babysits*) for the Monroe family.

10. Each of those books (*has, have*) (*their, its*) own special style.

## For Special Handling

When more than one verb is used in a sentence or paragraph, the time or tense must be consistent. Read the following paragraph.

> Yesterday, I interviewed several applicants for the administrative assistant position. The first woman walks into my office, sits down at the head of the conference table, and began interrogating me about affirmative action. I sit there staring until she finishes, and then say, "Thank you for an informative discussion," stand up, and showed her to the door.

*Yesterday,* sets the paragraph in the past. All verbs should remain in that tense. Damon Runyon can get away with telling a story that occurred in the past in the present tense. We ordinary folks can't. Damon Runyon was consistent, too. His story stayed in the present. It didn't flop back and forth. See the correct version below:

> Yesterday, I interviewed several applicants for the administrative assistant position. The first woman *walked* into my office, *sat* down at the head of the conference table, and *began* interrogating me about affirmative action. I *sat* there staring until she *finished,* and then *said,* "Thank you for an informative discussion," *stood* up, and *showed* her the door.

## For Special Handling

When writing or speaking, people can easily change *person*; in other words jump from second to third person pronouns:

> People should schedule important meetings early in the day because you are more alert during the early part of the work day.

The pronoun *you* refers to people. The correct pronoun would be *they*. Look at the next example.

> One should button your jacket when giving a formal presentation.

The correction? Here it is:

> One should button *one's* (or *his/her*) jacket when giving a formal presentation.

If *you* start, *you* finish. Compare the following:

Incorrect: You can't enter the Senate Chamber unless someone has a pass.
Correct: You can't enter the Senate Chamber unless *you* have a pass.

## PRACTICE 3

Correct the following paragraphs or sentences to keep tense and "people" consistent.

1. I enjoyed meeting you at the sales conference last week. Yours is one of the finest presentations I've seen on assertive marketing. My local managers and I benefit a great deal from your concrete illustrations of effective practices.

2. Mary's typing is excellent but, I don't know if one's shorthand is polished enough for the demands of this job.

3. Sometimes, even the most talented person in a department needs some guidance and benefited from the assistance of others.

4. When the senior partner of the firm makes a suggestion, everyone accepted it without question.

5. You must request vacation time in writing if one wants your request to be considered.

6. The agenda for the week includes two luncheon meetings and highlighted six departmental reports.

7. Whenever someone asks Marty for directions to the new plant, they get the roundabout route.

8. If anyone wants to work overtime, they should talk to Jeff in the front office.

9. I researched the material, organized it, and wrote the final report. I completed that paper with such satisfaction, and all I get is a C+.

10. Current training programs are not as successful as they could have been.

# Modifiers

Place modifiers (descriptive words and phrases) where they belong. They belong as close as possible to the word they are describing.

Some classic examples of misplaced modifiers are:

> Throw me down the stairs my coat.
> Throw Momma from the train a kiss.

What happened? In the first sentence, what should be thrown? My coat. Where should it be thrown? Down the stairs. To whom should it be thrown? Me.

> Throw my coat down the stairs to me.

In the second sentence, what should be thrown? A kiss. From where should it be thrown? The train. To whom should it be thrown? Momma.

> Throw a kiss from the train to Momma.

Sometimes, rearranging words alone will not help a sentence make sense.

> I often run to the store wearing my slippers.

Here is a possible change:

> *Wearing my slippers, I often run to the store.*

This is not the best correction. Here's another:

> *I often run to the store while wearing my slippers.*

The addition of the word *while* changes the sentence.

### PRACTICE 4

Rewrite the following paragraph, correcting misplaced modifiers.

Mr. Johnson stood in the hall a new water cooler. He believes that having the cooler in the hall will relieve traffic problems in the reception area. Most salesmen congregate at water coolers on their way to meetings. The receptionist called this problem to Mr. Johnson's attention at a meeting of water cooler congregants.

# Pronouns

Many people are easily confused by pronouns. The rules for correct usage are easy to master. There are pronouns that *act,* those that *receive action,* and those that *own.*

| Pronouns that act | Pronouns that receive action | Pronouns that own |
|---|---|---|
| I | me | my, mine |
| you | you | your, yours |
| he, she, it | him, her | his, her, hers, its |
| we | us | our, ours |
| they | them | their, theirs |
| who | whom | whose |

Now, let's see them in context.

> Mary and I (not *me*) found last year's seminar more valuable than this year's.
> I gave John and him (not *he*) the first lunch.
> I am very concerned about the effect *your* (not *you*) smoking will have on my health.
> *Whom* (not *who*) can we blame?

Often, pronoun errors are made when the pronoun appears with a noun.

> *Elsie and I share an apartment.*

You would not say "me share," so you would not say *"Elsie and me share."* Remember the purpose of the pronoun in the sentence. If it is performing an action, it must come from the action column on the chart. Sometimes people think action pronouns sound more correct. Have you heard this one?

> *John gave the keys to he and I.*

The pronouns in this sentence are receiving the action and, therefore, should be *him and me.* He and I must *do* the giving.

## For Special Handling

Sometimes you have to complete a sentence in your head to choose the right pronoun.

> John is a better programmer than I (am).

Once you add the *am,* you won't make the mistake of saying:

> John is a better programmer than me (am).

## For Special Handling

When you talk about someone's smoking, jogging, typing, cooking, etc., you are talking about a *thing,* not an action. So, you wouldn't say,

>*Mary hates him smoking.*

You would say,

>Mary hates his smoking.

Just remember to use the pronoun that means ownership in these cases.

## PRACTICE 5

Select the correct word to complete each sentence.

1. David and (*I, me*) are going to the outdoor concert.
2. Those reports are for Robert and (*I, me*).
3. (*We, Us*) and (*they, them*) are meeting at McDonald's at 6.
4. (*Who, Whom*) called while I was at the meeting?
5. Did you buy a wedding gift for Jose and (*she, her*)?
6. To (*who, whom*) should I send these invitations?
7. The company baseball team wants Sarah and (*I, me*) to join next season.
8. Gina understands the new office equipment better than (*I, me*).
9. Is that parking place ours or (*theirs, their's*).
10. I am very concerned about (*your, you're*) not keeping a record of expenses.

## More About Pronouns

Clarity in writing demands that pronoun references be clear. Your reader needs to know which noun the pronoun refers to. If that isn't immediately evident, the reader has to search back and forth over the sentence, trying to tie the pronoun to a previous word. Searching delays meaning.

>Although Rizzo recently joined Winston on the project, *he* will still report to the president.

Who is *he*? Rizzo? Winston? Here's the correction:

>Although Rizzo recently joined Winston on the project, *Winston* will still report to the president.

And another example:

> Marlene told Judy she was tired and wouldn't go to the meeting.

Who is tired? Marlene? Judy? It is clearer as:

> Marlene, feeling tired, decided not to go to the meeting. Marlene told Judy so.

Or:

> Because she was tired, Marlene told Judy she wouldn't go to the meeting.

Yet another example:

> He dropped the calculator on the glass-topped desk and broke it.

What broke? The calculator? The desk? It is better as:

> He dropped the calculator on the glass-topped desk. The glass broke.

Or

> He dropped the calculator on the glass-topped desk, breaking the glass.

Avoid using a pronoun for which there is no clear reference. Beware of sentences that begin with *this,* because the tendency is to forget that *this* must relate to something else.

> No: We sold more machinery than anyone else in the field. *This* helped us gain national recognition.
>
> Yes: We sold more machinery than anyone else in the field. Our *sales* helped us gain national recognition.

Avoid placing a pronoun too far from the word to which it refers. The meaning — the connection — will not be clear.

> The graph at the end of the report was included in *its* original format.

To what does *its* refer? The report? The graph? Place *its* close to *graph,* the word to which *its* refers.

> The graph, in its original format, was included at the end of the report.

## PRACTICE 6

In the following sentences, correct the errors in pronoun usage.

1. As each director arrives at the meeting, give them a financial statement.

2. Jan wrote the agenda with Betty, but she was ill and couldn't attend the meeting.

3. We wrote the sales presentation and produced the manual. It was a long one.

4. Before word processors, managers had to wait for his secretary to type a memo, but now managers find that they shorten the time it takes to send a message from one office to another.

5. Do not touch the magnetic surface of the diskette. This is so the oil from your fingertips won't get into the small holes in the plastic jacket.

# Run-on Sentences

A run-on sentence occurs when two complete thoughts are joined together, or run on, without correct punctuation.

> Most Scots are descended from their invaders these invaders included Celts, Norsemen, and Romans.

> Scotland has a population of over 5 million people three-fourths of the people live in the crowded Central Lowlands.

To correct a run-on sentence you have several choices:

1. You can decide to have two separate sentences.

> Most Scots are descended from their invaders. These invaders included Celts, Norsemen, and Romans.

2. If the thoughts are closely related, you can join the two with a semicolon.

> Most Scots are descended from their invaders; these invaders included Celts, Norsemen, and Romans.

3. You can join the sentences with a comma and a word that coordinates the two thoughts. Choose from these words: *and, but, or, for, not, yet, so.*

> Scotland has a population of over 5 million, but three-fourths of the people live in the crowded Central Lowlands.

4. Finally, you can combine both thoughts, having only one subject and verb for the sentence.

Most Scots are descended from their invaders, including the Celts, Norsemen, and Romans.

## PRACTICE 7

Correct these run-on sentences.

1. You'll have to discuss your vacation time with the personnel department they make the vacation schedule.
2. I'm a student at Michigan State University my major is in engineering.
3. When you make a recommendation, describe the present situation consider other courses of action.
4. Dr. Malcolm Brown has been named Chief of Surgery Dr. Susan Lovett has become Medical Director.
5. Communication between lawyer and client is privileged so is communication between doctor and patient.

# Sentence Fragments

In most circumstances you will use complete sentences. We say *most* because there are times when it isn't so. For example in conversation, we frequently use sentence fragments or even just single words.

"Ready?"
"Now?"
"Yes?"

In fiction, a series of fragments creates a special effect.

*There.* I finally found grandfather. *Still wearing the same grey coat. The same shabby hat.*

You understand from the context that grandfather was still wearing the same grey coat, the same shabby hat. The italic portions, however, are not complete sentences. They cannot stand independently, as complete sentences can. Occasionally, even in memos, letters, and reports, the writer may use a fragment to emphasize a point or to change the pace.

*One more suggestion.* Don't forget to attach your bills when you request repayment.

But when fragments appear again and again in business communications or school reports, they lose their punch. The reader can conclude only that the writer can't distinguish between a sentence fragment and a complete sentence.

What is a sentence fragment? A sentence fragment is a group of words that does not meet the minimum sentence requirements.

I saw him. *Standing at the water cooler.*

The first of the two sentences satisfies minimum sentence requirements.

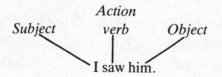

The second sentence, however, does not have a subject. The sentence does not tell *who was standing* at the water cooler. In fact, this fragment depends upon the sentence which comes before it for its meaning. That gives us the second part of the definition of a sentence fragment: a group of words that is dependent and, as such, depends upon an independent thought for completion. Let's look at that sentence, in corrected form.

I saw him standing at the water cooler.

By attaching *standing at the water cooler* to the independent thought, the writer has formed a complete sentence.

Sometimes a group of words looks like a complete sentence but, in fact, it is a clause. A *clause* is a group of words that has a subject and a verb; but not all clauses are complete sentences.

Home heating costs have gone up. *Because the cost of oil has risen sharply.*

Notice that the group of words in italics has a subject (*cost*) and a verb (*has risen*). But this clause cannot stand alone; it depends upon the previous thought for completion. Unless it is corrected, it remains a sentence fragment.

Be alert for words that introduce dependent clauses. (A dependent clause is one which cannot stand on its own.)

Examples of such words are:

| | | | | |
|---|---|---|---|---|
| after | if | when | whom | which |
| although | while | who | whose | that |

These words may signal that you've written a sentence fragment unless they are used properly.

## PRACTICE 8

Join the dependent clause to the independent clause, or rewrite the clause to make it independent.

1. The project director walked out of the meeting. Which was his way of avoiding the disagreement.
2. I try to counsel him about his work problems. When he needs my help.
3. Meet us at the worksite. After you return from the bank.
4. Some of the orders are sent directly to our customers. While others are picked up at the plant.
5. We'll send the order directly to you. That being the case.

## SUMMING IT UP

Apply what you've learned in this chapter to correct the following sentences.

1. We've just hired Daniel Callaghan. Whom we've known for several years.
2. Tom Redding told us that you are buying XYZ Corporation, we wish you success with your new venture.
3. The operator connects the calls by pushing a button. Using the Light-Up switchboard.
4. The thalamus fornix and mammillary body make memory possible. They are parts of the brain.
5. Either the underchefs or the head chef plan the meals.
6. Scientists now need to learn why the cells that control the disease dies.
7. Dick is a more likely candidate than me.
8. The boss told me about you oversleeping.
9. All of my coworkers has the combination to the safe.
10. Either Jack or one of the superintendents opens the door each morning.

# ANSWERS

## PRACTICE 1

The subway platform is very crowded to 8 a.m. Tourists (*rush*) to get started early. Many of the businessmen and women (*attempt*) to get to their offices before 9 a.m., and workers returning from the 12 a.m. shift also (*crowd*) the platform. One of the conductors (*is*) especially interesting to watch during this hectic time. He (*shouts*) directions and (*signals*) with his hands as though he were a performer in a Broadway show. Crowds of people (*stop*) in their haste to observe this showman. One of the commuters (*offers*) coffee to him each morning. Without skipping a beat, he (*accepts*) it with a wink of thanks.

## PRACTICE 2

1. Everyone *works* at his/her own pace.
2. Any of these dresses *is* suitable for that occasion.
3. John and he often *go* to Tilli's for lunch.
4. Few men *have* done this job as well as Martin.
5. Either of those courses *meets* the requirement.
6. Either Arnold or John *owns* that Honda.
7. Several of the office clerks *know* how to access the computer.
8. None of those posters *belongs* in this room.
9· Either Felice or her cousins *babysit* for the Monroe family.
10. Each of those books *has its* own special style.

## PRACTICE 3

The circled word in each sentence or paragraph sets the tense or person.
1. I (enjoyed) meeting you at the sales conference last week. Yours *was* one of the finest presentations I've seen on assertive marketing. My local managers and I *benefited* a great deal from your concrete illustrations of effective practices.
2. (Mary's) typing is excellent, but I don't know if *her* shorthand is polished enough for the demands of this job.
3. Sometimes, even the most talented person in a department (needs) some guidance and *benefits* from the assistance of others.
4. When the senior partner of the firm (makes) a suggestion, everyone *accepts* it without question.
5. (You) must request vacation time in writing if *you want* your request to be considered.
6. The agenda for the week (includes) two luncheon meetings and *highlights* six departmental reports.
7. Whenever (someone) asks Marty for directions to the new plant, *he/she gets* the roundabout route.
8. If (anyone) wants to work overtime, *he/she* should talk to Jeff in the front office.
9. I (researched) the material, organized it, and wrote the final report. I completed that paper with such satisfaction, and all I *got was* a C+.
10. Current training programs (are) not as successful as they could *be*.

## PRACTICE 4

Mr. Johnson stood a new water cooler in the hall. He believes that having the cooler in the hall will relieve traffic problems in the reception area. Most salesmen on their way to meetings congregate at water coolers. The receptionist called this problem of water cooler congregants to Mr. Johnson's attention at a meeting.

## PRACTICE 5

1. David and *I* are going to the outdoor concert.
2. Those reports are for Robert and *me*.
3. *We* and *they* are meeting at McDonald's at 6.
4. *Who* called while I was at the meeting?
5. Did you buy a wedding gift for Jose and *her*?
6. To *whom* should I send these invitations?
7. The company baseball team wants Sarah and *me* to join next season.
8. Gina understands the new office equipment better than *I*.
9. Is that parking place ours or *theirs*?
10. I am very concerned about *your* not keeping a record of expenses.

## PRACTICE 6

1. As each director arrives at the meeting, give him/her a financial statement.
2. Jan wrote the agenda with Betty, but Betty was ill and couldn't attend the meeting.
3. We wrote the sales presentation and produced the long manual.
4. Before word processors, managers had to wait for a secretary to type a memo, but now managers find that the word processors shorten the time it takes to send a message from one office to another.
5. Do not touch the magnetic surface of the diskette. Careful handling will prevent the oil from your fingertips from getting into the small holes in the plastic jacket.

## PRACTICE 7

Answers Will Vary.
1. You'll have to discuss your vacation time with the Personnel Department; they make the vacation schedule.
2. I'm a student at Michigan State University, majoring in engineering.
3. When you make a recommendation, describe the present situation and consider other courses of action.
4. Dr. Malcolm Brown has been named Chief of Surgery; Dr. Susan Lovett has become Medical Director.
5. Just as communication between lawyer and client is privileged, so is communication between doctor and patient.

## PRACTICE 8

Answers Will Vary.
1. To avoid the disagreement, the project director walked out of the meeting.
2. I try to counsel him about his work problems when he needs my help.
3. Meet us at the work site after you return from the bank.
4. Some of the orders are sent directly to our customers, while others are picked up at the plant.
5. We'll send the order directly to you, that being the case.

## SUMMING IT UP

Answers Will Vary.
1. We've just hired Daniel Callaghan whom we've known for several years.
2. Tom Redding told us that you are buying XYZ Corporation. We wish you success with your new venture.
3. The operator connects the calls by pushing a button, using the Light-Up switchboard.

4. Thalamus, fornix, and mammillary body, all parts of the brain, make memory possible.
5. Either the underchefs or the head chef plans the meal.
6. Scientists now need to learn why the cells that control the disease die.
7. Dick is a more likely candidate than I.
8. The boss told me about your oversleeping.
9. All of my coworkers have the combination to the safe.
10. Either Jack or one of the superintendents open the door each morning.

# 10.

# Being a Good Mechanic

---

Books have been written on capitalization and punctuation. In this chapter we give you a review of just the basic rules and a brief overview of the major problems most writers have.

You probably know that a sentence begins with a capital letter and ends with a period, an exclamation point, or a question mark. But most of us encounter problems between that first capital letter and the end mark. What words should be capitalized? When do you use a comma, a semicolon, a colon? Learning a few basic rules will help you answer these questions — and improve your writing skills.

## The Comma

1. A comma separates two complete thoughts joined by a conjunction such as *and, but, or, nor,* or *for.*

   *We moved* our offices to the sixteenth floor, and *we forgot* to bring all the wastebaskets.

   If each part of the sentence did not have a subject and a verb, the comma would be left out.

   *We moved* our offices to the sixteenth floor and *forgot* to bring all the wastebaskets.

2. An introductory word or group of words is usually followed by a comma.

   *Generally,* it is easier to get a job if you've had work experience.

   To complete the project, we had to work on the weekend.

   *Since you will be working until 10 p.m.,* you may come in at 11 a.m. today.

If the sentence is turned around, the comma is left out.

You may come in at 11 a.m. today since you will be working until 10 p.m.

3. Commas set off words or groups of words that interrupt the flow of the sentence.

The board of directors, *however,* will not approve the merger.

Edmond Simpson, *the president of the local board of education,* has done a great deal for our schools.

4. Commas separate three or more items in a series. A comma should come before the *and* between the last two items.

Please order four dozen manilla envelopes, letter-size file folders, *and* a thousand ball point pens.

5. A comma separates the day from the year and the year from the rest of the sentence.

Lena began working on May 15, 1981, at the Positive Insurance Company's main office.

The date on a letter or memo would have this form:

June 23, 1978

6. A comma separates the name of a city from the name of the state and the name of the state from the rest of the sentence.

My next business trip is to *Detroit***,** *Michigan***,** and *Orlando***,** *Florida.*

In the inside address of a letter, the city and state would be separated by a comma. No punctuation comes between the state and the zip code.

Groton, Massachusetts 01450
San Diego, CA 92101

7. A comma is used after the greeting in a friendly letter.

Dear Walter,

8. A comma follows the closing in a friendly letter or a business letter.

Very truly yours,
William Baez

9. A comma separates a direct quotation from the rest of the sentence.

"I put the file on the desk," the assistant said. The manager answered, "I'll look at it in a moment."

# The Semicolon

1. The semicolon connects two complete thoughts that are closely related. Sometimes a word such as *however, nevertheless,* or *therefore* follows the semicolon.

The dinner was excellent; the service was awful.
Ms. Steinberg liked your proposal; *however,* she cannot commit any more money at this time.

2. The semicolon is used for clarity to separate complete thoughts that contain commas.

Since he arrived, my uncle has broken our coffee pot, the sofa bed, and the washing machine; but we really enjoy his company.

# Quotation Marks

1. Quotation marks separate the exact words of the speaker from the person who spoke them.

The manager said, "Is your plan feasible considering our resources?"

Note that the question mark is placed inside the quotation marks because it is part of the question being quoted.

2. Quotation marks also set off both parts of a broken quotation. Don't capitalize the first word of the second part of the quotation unless it is the beginning of a new sentence.

"Once we've looked at your application," the admissions officer said, "we'll either accept you immediately or send you a deferral statement."

"We've looked at your application," the admissions officer said. "We'll either accept you immediately or send you a deferral statement."

Note the period *inside* the quotation marks at the end of the second sentence. This is customary.

# The Colon

1. The colon is used to introduce a list (when the list is not preceded by a verb).

   Please review the following factors: costs for the month, expenses for the month, and nonmonetary benefits for the month.

2. The colon is used after the greeting in a business letter.

   Dear Ms. McMillan:

# The Hyphen

1. The hyphen is used to divide a word at the end of a line. Always divide a word between syllables. Use your dictionary to help you.

   Everyone in our department stays on Thurs-
   days for the exercise class.

2. The hyphen divides compound numbers from *twenty-one* to *ninety-nine*.

   thirty-six, seventy-eight

3. The hyphen links two or more words to form a compound adjective.

   *well-respected* teacher
   *free-floating* currencies

4. The hyphen is used when adding some prefixes.

   ex-wife    vice-president    non-European

# The Apostrophe

1. An apostrophe shows that one or more letters have been omitted in a contraction.

   Janet *isn't* (is not) studying tonight.
   *We'll* (we will) call you at six o'clock.

2.  An apostrophe shows possession. The apostrophe comes *before* the *s* in singular words and *after* the *s* in plural words. Exceptions are words made plural without an *s*.

> Marie's jacket
> the baby's rattle (singular)
> the babies' rattles (plural)
> the administrator's meeting (singular)
> the administrators' meeting (plural)
> the woman's shoe (singular)
> the women's shoes (plural)
> the child's food (singular)
> the children's food (plural)

3.  An apostrophe shows the plural of letters and numbers.

> All *4*'s are on the far court.
> I never get *E*'s when I play scrabble.

# Dashes

Dashes emphasize an interruption within a sentence.

> We planned the reception — a beautiful one — right after the ceremony.

# Parentheses

Parentheses set off words not directly related to the main thought of the sentence. The information in parentheses is sometimes thought of as an "aside."

The lock on the front door (as you know) must be fixed.

The correspondence has been entered in the files (look under drawers A–K).

**PRACTICE 1**

Correctly punctuate each of the following sentences. Some sentences have more than one error. Some have no errors. If a sentence is correct, write C.

1.  Before leaving the office Mr. Bondino reviewed all of the days cases.

2.  He and I work for the same company and we take the train together.

3. The chief administrator had wanted to interview Joan but was unable to keep the appointment.

4. It isn't that we dont want to join you we just cant.

5. "If I had known you were serving dinner" said Beth, I would not have eaten.

6. Martin Haber my exboss was at the dinner.

7. When you arrive at the airport in Seattle Washington please give me a call.

8. Gregory Tesides the Symphony Club president and his wife a librarian chaired the benefit for the local hospital.

## PRACTICE 2

Correctly punctuate each of the following sentences. Some sentences have more than one error. Look carefully for all possible items of punctuation.

1. The word processor can identify all the number 6s in the report.

2. While many people are concerned about minor pollutants such as solid waste the more serious problem of toxic waste has surfaced.

3. College costs have risen to an all time high said Chancellor White.

4. Motivation is not enough you must earn better grades.

5. Although Clara had expected some problems her new job as the presidents assistant is challenging and rewarding.

6. That woman the one in the yellow dress is Sarahs mother.

7. William isnt working tonight but Keith will substitute for him.

8. Did you read the article about self styled nutrition experts?

9. When you are in Lincoln Nebraska you can visit a friend of mine.

10. Chuck Hardwick our local assemblyman is a very responsive and responsible legislator.

11. Some legislators however respond to mail only with form letters.

12. The shipment did arrive on time however several items we had ordered were not included.

13. I wont ask you again forget it.

14. If you thought thirty nine was a difficult birthday wait until you are forty nine.

15. Our department cant run effectively without the following supplies file folders address labels envelopes pencils a pencil sharpener and felt tip pens.

**PRACTICE 3**

Supply the missing punctuation in the following business letter.

July 12 1985

Ms. Alice Smith
Wilson Supply Company
419 West Broad Street
Westfield New Jersey 07090

Dear Ms. Smith

Since you and I spoke on June 24 I have decided to give our office supply order to your company. I assume that the terms we discussed during that conversation still apply.

Instead of waiting for your official order form I will place our order now. Please send us the following items

3 reams of 20 lb. paper
6 dozen pencils number 2s
1 box of Smiths Erasable Bond

Thank you for your immediate attention to this order.
I look forward to our working together. By the way the next time you are in our part of town with samples please call me.

Sincerely
Mary Ellen Collins

# A Few Rules of Capitalization

The following items should be capitalized:

1. The first letter of the first word in a sentence

   **P**lease complete the application today.

2. The first word of a direct quotation

   Ms. Selletti replied, "**W**e have finished the report."

3. The word *I*

Yesterday **I** spoke to the manager.

4. Names of persons, places, streets, organizations, languages, specific school courses, important historical events, and documents

My friend **Juanita Lee** lives on **Kingston Street**, in **Cleveland**, **Illinois**. She is president of the **American Cancer Society** in her community, speaks **Spanish** fluently, and teaches **Modern History II** at **Wilson High School**.

The **Emancipation Proclamation** was signed during the **Civil War**.

**Thomas Tsing**, manager of the **Personnel Department** at the **Savalot Corporation**, has been appointed to the company's **Health and Safety Committee**.

5. A brand name, but *not* the word that identifies the product

I went to the drugstore to buy some **Smoothmore** toothpaste and **Flexo** shampoo.

6. Days of the week, months, holidays

Next **Monday**, **May 30**, will be **Memorial Day**.

The names of the seasons are usually *not* capitalized.

I will graduate next *summer*.

7. *East, west, north,* and *south* when they designate sections of the country or are part of a place name, but *not* when they simply indicate direction.

I love the **West**. When traveling *west* on Route 80, watch for the radar traps.

She lives on **South Bellview Drive**.

8. The first word and each important word in a title of a book, play, magazine, poem, or other work

Ernest Hemingway's novel ***A Farewell to Arms*** will always be my favorite.

9. The initials of a person's name

**J. C.** Walinski
Maria **K.** Sukihani

10. A personal title *only* when it comes before the name

Robert Kerry became *captain* after **C**aptain Healey retired.

Last week **M**rs. Laurel Golden was named *president* of the Red Cross. She was congratulated by **D**r. Steven Jackson, the *secretary-treasurer* of the organization.

11. The first word in each line of poetry

**H**e walked amongst the trial men
**I**n a suit of shabby gray. . . .

12. The names of the Deity

**G**od    Allah

## PRACTICE 4

To correct these sentences, either add or delete capital letters.

1. Our company, Ralme, inc., moved its headquarters to Carson city, Nevada, in the Spring of 1982.

2. We've asked Mr. Arthur Ralme to chair the Board of directors of Hewes Corporation.

3. After we leave San Francisco, we'll travel in the orient for two weeks.

4. Submit your bid to the department of transportation, Washington, D.C.

5. First walk east on Main Street until you reach east fourth Avenue.

6. Have you read the new book on management, *Making time make you money*?

## PRACTICE 5

In the following instructions for taking telephone orders, supply the missing capital letters; remove the unnecessary ones.

1. answer each call as quickly as possible.

2. Determine that the caller is a Member.
    a. Ask the caller for his/her name and address.
    b. Insert facts into the Computer.
    c. Ask the caller for his/her Membership Number and expiration Date.
    d. Check these details with the Computer printout.

3. Take the order. Enter the Order into the computer.

4. Repeat the Order to the Customer.

These instructions take effect on february 1.

## PRACTICE 6

Correct any capitalization errors in the following letter.

January 10, 1986

Mr. Henry Grumman
67 Main street
Wilmington, Delaware 19823

Dear Mr. Grumman:

We are happy to confirm your family's Reservations for February 22–26, and are delighted to welcome you again this year. You requested two rooms on the Second Floor which we will reserve for you.

Since last year, we've added many Winter Sports Activities. I'm sending you our new brochure, which describes these activities. I know that your family in particular will enjoy the night skiing.

If I can do anything else to help you plan your Vacation, please let me know.

sincerely,

Marge Browning

# ANSWERS

## PRACTICE 1

1. Before leaving the office, Mr. Bondino reviewed all of the day's cases.
2. He and I work for the same company, and we take the train together.
3. Correct.
4. It isn't that we don't want to join you; we just can't.
5. "If I had known you were serving dinner," said Beth, "I would not have eaten."
6. Martin Haber, my ex-boss, was at the dinner.
7. When you arrive at the airport in Seattle, Washington, please give me a call.
8. Gregory Tesides, the Symphony Club president, and his wife, a librarian, chaired the benefit for the local hospital.

## PRACTICE 2

1. The word processor can identify all the number 6's in the report.
2. While many people are concerned about minor pollutants such as solid waste, the more serious problem of toxic waste has surfaced.
3. "College costs have risen to an all-time high," said Chancellor White.
4. Motivation is not enough; you must earn better grades.
5. Although Clara had expected some problems, her new job as the president's assistant is challenging and rewarding.
6. That woman—the one in the yellow dress—is Sarah's mother. [or That woman (the one in the yellow dress) is Sarah's mother.]
7. William isn't working tonight, but Keith will substitute for him.
8. Did you read the article about self-styled nutrition experts?
9. When you are in Lincoln, Nebraska, you can visit a friend of mine.
10. Chuck Hardwick, our local assemblyman, is a very responsive and responsible legislator.
11. Some legislators, however, respond to mail only with form letters.
12. The shipment did arrive on time; however, several items we had ordered were not included.
13. I won't ask you again; forget it.
14. If you thought thirty-nine was a difficult birthday, wait until you are forty-nine.
15. Our department can't run effectively without the following supplies: file folders, address labels, envelopes, pencils, a pencil sharpener, and felt-tip pens.

## PRACTICE 3

July 12, 1985

Ms. Alice Smith
Wilson Supply Company
419 West Broad Street
Westfield, New Jersey 07090

Dear Ms. Smith:

Since you and I spoke on June 24, I have decided to give our office supply order to your company. I assume that the terms we discussed during that conversation still apply.

Instead of waiting for your official order form, I will place our order now. Please send us the following items:

3 reams of 20 lb. paper
6 dozen pencils (number 2's)
1 box of Smith's Erasable Bond

Thank you for your immediate attention to this order.

I look forward to our working together. By the way, the next time you are in our part of town with samples, please call me.

Sincerely,

Mary Ellen Collins

## PRACTICE 4

1. Our company, Ralme, Inc., moved its headquarters to Carson City, Nevada, in the spring of 1982.
2. We've asked Mr. Arthur Ralme to chair the Board of Directors of Hewes Corporation.
3. After we leave San Francisco, we'll travel in the Orient for two weeks.
4. Submit your bid to the Department of Transportation, Washington, D.C.
5. First walk east on Main Street until you reach East Fourth Avenue.
6. Have you read the new book on management, *Making Time Make You Money*?

## PRACTICE 5

1. Answer each call as quickly as possible.
2. Determine that the caller is a member.
   a. Ask the caller for his/her name and address.
   b. Insert facts into the computer.
   c. Ask the caller for his/her membership number and expiration date.
   d. Check these details with the computer printout.
3. Take the order. Enter the order into the computer.
4. Repeat the order to the customer.
   These instructions take effect on February 1.

# PRACTICE 6

January 10, 1986

Mr. Henry Grumman
67 Main Street
Wilmington, Delaware 19823

Dear Mr. Grumman:

We are happy to confirm your family's reservations for February 22–26, and are delighted to welcome you again this year. You requested two rooms on the second floor which we will reserve for you.

Since last year, we've added many winter sports activities. I'm sending you our new brochure, which describes these activities. I know that your family in particular will enjoy the night skiing.

If I can do anything else to help you plan your vacation, please let me know.

Sincerely,

Marge Browning

# 11.

# Sharpening the Tools of Your Trade

## Spelling

For some people, correct spelling seems to come easily. For many others, spelling correctly takes persistent study. If you have trouble with spelling, try this approach to improve:

1. Use a small notebook to record the words you frequently misspell.
2. When you discover a problem word, write it in your notebook. Check a dictionary for the correct spelling, syllable division, and pronunciation.
3. Look at the word. Say it in syllables.
4. Try to apply one of the rules that follow to understand why the word is spelled as it is.
5. Close your eyes and picture the word.
6. Write the word. Check it. Rewrite it.
7. Review words you have already studied.

Learning to spell a long word is much easier if you divide it into syllables. For example:

con • tin • u • a • tion

Learn to spell each syllable and, finally, put the word together.

### Adding Prefixes and Suffixes

Spelling problems sometimes occur when prefixes and suffixes are added to words. A *prefix* is a group of letters added to the *beginning* of a word to change its meaning. A *suffix* is a group of letters added to the *end* of a word to change its meaning. Sometimes the word to which a prefix or suffix is added is called the *root* word. For example:

| Prefix | Root | Suffix |
|--------|------|--------|
| *dis*quiet | quiet | quiet*ly* |

Most often, prefixes can be added to a word without changing the spelling of the root word. For example:

| Prefix | (Meaning) | Word | Combination |
|--------|-----------|------|-------------|
| un = | (not) | necessary = | unnecessary |
| ir = | (not) | reversible = | irreversible |

## PRACTICE 1

Add a prefix from the list below to each of the words in the exercise.

| in– | re– | ir– | ac– | de– | co– |
|-----|-----|-----|-----|-----|-----|
| mal– | im– | mis– | un– | dis– | il– |

1. _____nutrition
2. _____education
3. _____appropriate
4. _____reverent
5. _____patient
6. _____legal

7. _____inform
8. _____available
9. _____assemble
10. ___pay
11. _____personalize
12. _____climate

A suffix that begins with a consonant doesn't change the spelling of most words. (A *consonant* is any letter that is not a vowel.) The vowels are *a, e, i, o,* and *u.* For example:

    mortal + ly     = mortally
    like + ness     = likeness

But there are some exceptions:

    true + ly       = truly
    due + ly        = duly

When you add a suffix beginning with a vowel to a word that ends in a consonant, the spelling of the root word usually doesn't change. For example:

    port + able     = portable
    economic + al   = economical

Suffixes *do* change the spelling of words that end in *y*: the *y* changes to *i*. For example:

$$
\begin{aligned}
\text{defy} + \text{ance} &= \text{defiance} \\
\text{necessary} + \text{ly} &= \text{necessarily}
\end{aligned}
$$

When you add a suffix that begins with a vowel to a word that ends in *e*, drop the final *e*. For example:

$$
\begin{aligned}
\text{announce} + \text{ing} &= \text{announcing} \\
\text{continue} + \text{ous} &= \text{continuous}
\end{aligned}
$$

Exceptions are words that end in *–ge* or *–ce*. They keep the final *e* to maintain the soft sound of the *g* or *c*. For example:

$$
\begin{aligned}
\text{change} + \text{able} &= \text{changeable} \\
\text{notice} + \text{able} &= \text{noticeable}
\end{aligned}
$$

Another exception is

$$
\text{dye} + \text{ing} = \text{dyeing}
$$

## PRACTICE 2

For each item add the suffix to the word to make a new word. Use your dictionary to help you.

| | WORD | SUFFIX | |
|---|---|---|---|
| 1. | announce | ment | = _____ |
| 2. | try | ing | = _____ |
| 3. | happy | ness | = _____ |
| 4. | associate | ion | = _____ |
| 5. | dispense | able | = _____ |
| 6. | definite | ly | = _____ |
| 7. | economic | al | = _____ |
| 8. | courage | ous | = _____ |
| 9. | move | able | = _____ |
| 10. | hearty | ly | = _____ |
| 11. | practical | ly | = _____ |
| 12. | port | able | = _____ |

| 13. | rude | ness | = | _____ |
| 14. | guide | ance | = | _____ |
| 15. | fulfill | ment | = | _____ |

## PRACTICE 3

Circle the number of the incorrectly spelled word in each group. If there is no error, circle number 5.

1. (1) unimportant  (2) revelation  (3) cumulative
   (4) irational  (5) no error

2. (1) brighter  (2) happyness  (3) unaccustomed
   (4) berate  (5) no error

3. (1) impossible  (2) cooperation  (3) inactive  (4) mispell
   (5) no error

4. (1) commencment  (2) coverage  (3) practically
   (4) extraction  (5) no error

5. (1) safty  (2) forgiveness  (3) shining  (4) amusement
   (5) no error

6. (1) becoming  (2) really  (3) plainness  (4) actually
   (5) no error

7. (1) adorable  (2) contagious  (3) acumulate  (4) supervise
   (5) no error

8. (1) loneliness  (2) personal  (3) barely  (4) noticable
   (5) no error

9. (1) continuation  (2) arguement  (3) ridiculous  (4) usage
   (5) no error

10. (1) surprised  (2) acquisitiveness  (3) carefully
    (4) virtuous  (5) no error

## Stress and Spelling Changes

A word that contains more than one syllable has stress on one of those syllables. For instance, say this word in syllables: *con • cep • tu • al*. One syllable is emphasized: the second. Its stress is marked in this way in a dictionary; *con • ceṕ • tu • al*. The stress is on the *cep* syllable. Stress is often a key to spelling.

## PRACTICE 4

In each word below, place a stress mark to show which syllable is emphasized. Use a dictionary to help you. The first word is done for you.

1. painť · er
2. pri · vate

3. of · fice
4. e · con · o · my

5. ad · vise
6. bal · ance
7. dis · sat · is · fy
8. de · vel · op · ment
9. in · di · vid · u · al
10. pre · fer

11. pref · er · ence
12. psy · chol · o · gy
13. vac · il · late
14. u · nan · i · mous
15. wretch · ed

When you add –*ed* or –*ing* or –*er* to a one-syllable word that ends in a consonant preceded by a vowel, double the final consonant. For example:

| | |
|---|---|
| plan | planned |
| set | setting |
| run | running |
| thin | thinner |

Double the final consonant when you add –*ed, –ing,* or –*ence* to a two-syllable word that ends in a consonant preceded by a vowel *and* whose second syllable is accented. For example:

| | |
|---|---|
| de · fer | de · ferred |
| oc · cur | oc · curred |
| oc · cur | oc · cur · rence |
| re · fer | re · fer · ring |

When you add –*ence* to a two-syllable word, do *not* double the final consonant if the accent in the new word is *not* on the second syllable. For example:

| | |
|---|---|
| re · fer | ref · er · ence |
| con · fer | con · fer · ence |
| pre · fer | pre · fer · ence |

## PRACTICE 5

Circle the number of the incorrectly spelled word in each group. If there is no error, circle number 5.

1. (1) referred   (2) preferrence   (3) stunning   (4) winding
   (5) no error
2. (1) batted   (2) conferred   (3) reference   (4) detered
   (5) no error
3. (1) binder   (2) funnier   (3) pictured   (4) reared
   (5) no error
4. (1) sunning   (2) preferable   (3) deterent   (4) banning
   (5) no error

5.  (1) preferred   (2) hitting   (3) fanned   (4) occurence
    (5) no error

## A Spelling Rhyme

Remember this one? Use *i* before *e* except after *c*. For example, *relief, receipt*. But there's an exception: Use *e* before *i* in words with a long–*a* sound (rhyme with *say*). For example, *neighbor, weigh*. Other exceptions to this basic rule are *weird, seize, either, leisure, neither*.

**PRACTICE 6**

Insert *ei* or *ie* to complete the following words.

1.  n____ce
2.  dec____ve
3.  th____f
4.  rel____ve
5.  n____gh

6.  rec____ve
7.  conc____ve
8.  bel____f
9.  n____ther
10. s____ze

## Forming Plurals

These are the rules for forming the plurals of words.

1.  Most words form plurals by adding *s*.

    | | |
    |---|---|
    | pencil | pencils |
    | tree | trees |
    | brochure | brochures |
    | computer | computers |

2.  Words ending in *y* preceded by a consonant form the plural by changing *y* to *i* and adding *es*.

    | | |
    |---|---|
    | sky | skies |
    | glory | glories |

    Note: If a vowel precedes a final *y*, the plural is formed by adding *s*.

    | | |
    |---|---|
    | monkey | monkeys |
    | stray | strays |

3.  Words ending in *o* preceded by a consonant form plurals by adding *es*.

    | | |
    |---|---|
    | tomato | tomatoes |
    | hero | heroes |

Musical words ending in *o* preceded by a consonant usually form the plural by adding only *s*.

| | |
|---|---|
| alto | altos |
| piano | pianos |

4. Words ending in *s, sh, ch,* and *x,* form the plural by adding *es*.

| | |
|---|---|
| boss | bosses |
| crush | crushes |
| porch | porches |
| tax | taxes |

5. A compound word forms its plural by adding *s* to the principal word.

| | |
|---|---|
| mother-in-law | mothers-in-law |
| forget-me-not | forget-me-nots |

6. Words ending in –*ful* form the plural by adding *s*.

| | |
|---|---|
| cupful | cupfuls |

7. Some words have the same spelling for the singular and the plural.

| | |
|---|---|
| one deer | two deer |
| one trout | two trout |
| one Chinese | two Chinese |
| one sheep | two sheep |

8. Some words form their plurals by special changes.

| | |
|---|---|
| thief | thieves |
| knife | knives |
| leaf | leaves |
| woman | women |
| child | children |
| tooth | teeth |
| louse | lice |
| crisis | crises |
| alumnus | alumni |
| datum | data |
| appendix | appendices (or appendixes) |

## PRACTICE 7

Circle the number of the incorrectly spelled word in each group. If there is no error, circle number 5. Use your dictionary to help you.

1. (1) geese    (2) mouthsful    (3) commanders-in-chief
   (4) men    (5) no error

2. (1) Japaneses    (2) bases    (3) echoes    (4) foxes
   (5) no error

3. (1) bacilli    (2) son-in-laws    (3) series
   (4) handkerchiefs    (5) no error

4. (1) feet    (2) properties    (3) passerby    (4) mice
   (5) no error

5. (1) wolfs    (2) dresses    (3) potatoes
   (4) vice-presidents    (5) no error

Following are rules regarding the word endings *sede, ceed,* and *cede.*

1. Only one word is spelled with a *sede* ending:

   supersede

2. Only three words are spelled with a *ceed* ending:

   succeed    exceed    proceed (to go forward)

3. All other words of this type are spelled with a *cede* ending. For example:

   precede (to go ahead of someone)    recede    concede

## *In Summary*

As we said at the beginning of this chapter, spelling correctly comes easily to some people but only with persistent study for others. For those who do need more practice, we have provided many review exercises in this spelling chapter. You may decide to do only three or four or five of these practices if you see that your score is ninety percent correct or better in each one. If your score is less than that, though, you should review the spelling rules and continue with the practices.

These exercises cover a variety of frequently misspelled words. Not every word is covered by a rule given above. If you decide that you need even more help in improving your spelling, study a book that is devoted totally to spelling. We've suggested several titles in the book list that follows the text.

## PRACTICE 8

Circle the number of the incorrectly spelled word in each group. If there is no error, circle number 5. Use your dictionary to help you.

1.  (1) acknowledge    (2) deception    (3) conclusivly
    (4) commodity    (5) no error
2.  (1) incurred    (2) coranation    (3) voluntary
    (4) herald    (5) no error
3.  (1) simular    (2) bulletin    (3) bored  (4) quizzes
    (5) no error
4.  (1) duchess    (2) achevement    (3) monarchs
    (4) fertile    (5) no error
5.  (1) distribute    (2) sieze    (3) premises
    (4) tonnage    (5) no error
6.  (1) monthly    (2) primarily    (3) condemned
    (4) dupped    (5) no error
7.  (1) cancellation    (2) derrick    (3) pertinant
    (4) utilize    (5) no error
8.  (1) nowadays    (2) courtesies    (3) negotiate
    (4) guardian    (5) no error
9.  (1) loot    (2) faculties    (3) lovly    (4) axle
    (5) no error
10. (1) fragrance    (2) accompanied    (3) preference
    (4) athletic    (5) no error

## PRACTICE 9

Circle the number of the incorrectly spelled word in each group. If there is no error, circle number 5. Use your dictionary to help you.

1.  (1) liquid  (2) disappear  (3) swirling  (4) dissolve
    (5) no error
2.  (1) inexorable  (2) mercyful  (3) capacity  (4) arboreal
    (5) no error
3.  (1) disolution  (2) agreeable  (3) rammed  (4) diseases
    (5) no error
4.  (1) minimize  (2) sophomore  (3) attorneys  (4) candidacy
    (5) no error
5.  (1) unnecessary  (2) carnage  (3) wierd  (4) judgment
    (5) no error
6.  (1) roses  (2) goverment  (3) absence  (4) churches
    (5) no error
7.  (1) emergency  (2) eager  (3) cordialy  (4) citizen
    (5) no error

8.  (1) benefit   (2) boxes   (3) consequence   (4) peice
    (5) no error
9.  (1) journey   (2) majority   (3) necessarily   (4) relief
    (5) no error
10. (1) yacht   (2) traveler   (3) profession   (4) accede
    (5) no error

## PRACTICE 10

Circle the number of the incorrectly spelled word in each group. If there is no error, circle number 5. Use your dictionary to help you.

1.  (1) overrate   (2) misapprehend   (3) habitualy
    (4) greenness   (5) no error
2.  (1) deferred   (2) roping   (3) approval   (4) applyance
    (5) no error
3.  (1) candys   (2) valleys   (3) torches   (4) files   (5) no error
4.  (1) immaterial   (2) dissapoint   (3) practically
    (4) unabated   (5) no error
5.  (1) embargos   (2) teeth   (3) radios   (4) sopranos
    (5) no error
6.  (1) preparing   (2) writing   (3) propeling   (4) controlled
    (5) no error
7.  (1) crises   (2) geese   (3) loaves   (4) trucksful   (5) no error
8.  (1) truely   (2) moving   (3) running   (4) famous
    (5) no error
9.  (1) shelves   (2) benches   (3) knives   (4) churches
    (5) no error
10. (1) salarys   (2) basketfuls   (3) reddest   (4) nameless
    (5) no error

## PRACTICE 11

Circle the incorrectly spelled word in each group. If there is no error, circle number 5. Use your dictionary to help you.

1.  (1) belief   (2) achieve   (3) neice   (4) weigh   (5) no error
2.  (1) yield   (2) neighbor   (3) deceive   (4) releif   (5) no error
3.  (1) benefited   (2) appealed   (3) refered   (4) equipped
    (5) no error
4.  (1) preference   (2) reference   (3) asessment   (4) colonel
    (5) no error
5.  (1) motivating   (2) humorous   (3) sophomore   (4) similar
    (5) no error
6.  (1) primarily   (2) adjustment   (3) preoccupy   (4) receit
    (5) no error

7. (1) aquired   (2) brief   (3) contemptible   (4) height
   (5) no error
8. (1) erred   (2) millionaire   (3) misanthrope   (4) lieutenent
   (5) no error
9. (1) adjournament   (2) caucus   (3) contagious
   (4) digestible   (5) no error
10. (1) carefuly   (2) calendar   (3) macaroni   (4) preceding
    (5) no error

## PRACTICE 12

Circle the number of the incorrectly spelled word in each group. If there is no error, circle number 5. Use your dictionary to help you.

1. (1) changeable   (2) athleletic   (3) grammar   (4) fortissimo
   (5) no error
2. (1) filial   (2) leisure   (3) temperture   (4) treachery
   (5) no error
3. (1) bulletin   (2) amendment   (3) incessent
   (4) kindergarten   (5) no error
4. (1) legitiment   (2) vivisection   (3) pervade   (4) courtesies
   (5) no error
5. (1) prefer   (2) preferred   (3) preference   (4) patrolled
   (5) no error
6. (1) ninth   (2) correspondent   (3) canoe   (4) hideous
   (5) no error
7. (1) apparently   (2) foreign   (3) carriage   (4) forfeit
   (5) no error
8. (1) aggregate   (2) massacre   (3) omissions   (4) tetnus
   (5) no error
9. (1) exceed   (2) intercede   (3) proceed   (4) procedure
   (5) no error
10. (1) fundimental   (2) misspell   (3) hypocrite
    (4) penitentiary   (5) no error

## PRACTICE 13

Circle the number of the incorrectly spelled word in each group. If there is no error, circle number 5. Use your dictionary to help you.

1. (1) torches   (2) salaries   (3) valleys   (4) shelves
   (5) no error
2. (1) absense   (2) gases   (3) accident   (4) capitalize
   (5) no error

3. (1) executive  (2) divide  (3) discusion  (4) eager
   (5) no error
4. (1) contrary  (2) atheletic  (3) critical  (4) banquet
   (5) no error
5. (1) association  (2) character  (3) earliest  (4) decide
   (5) no error
6. (1) Wenesday  (2) knives  (3) concerning
   (4) communicate  (5) no error
7. (1) appreciate  (2) except  (3) scene  (4) numerous
   (5) no error
8. (1) national  (2) posession  (3) industrious  (4) volume
   (5) no error
9. (1) patient  (2) quantity  (3) boundary  (4) probably
   (5) no error
10. (1) warrant  (2) laboratory  (3) interesting  (4) libary
    (5) no error

## PRACTICE 14

Circle the number of the incorrectly spelled word in each group. If there is no error, circle number 5. Use your dictionary to help you.

1. (1) biased  (2) aberation  (3) wholly  (4) vacuum
   (5) no error
2. (1) sensible  (2) ecstasy  (3) embarrass  (4) essential
   (5) no error
3. (1) asertain  (2) correlation  (3) abeyance  (4) diocese
   (5) no error
4. (1) fifth  (2) resileince  (3) nickel  (4) official
   (5) no error
5. (1) satellite  (2) originate  (3) illegitimate  (4) policy
   (5) no error
6. (1) subversive  (2) predatory  (3) lucritive  (4) prairie
   (5) no error
7. (1) pacifist  (2) senior  (3) source  (4) surfiet  (5) no error
8. (1) weild  (2) vacillate  (3) vengeance  (4) transaction
   (5) no error
9. (1) queue  (2) masquerade  (3) preside  (4) prohibit
   (5) no error
10. (1) psicology  (2) possession  (3) measurable
    (4) impeccable  (5) no error

**PRACTICE 15**

Circle the number of the incorrectly spelled word in each group. If there is no error, circle number 5. Use your dictionary to help you.

1. (1) derogatory   (2) neglagible   (3) rehearsal   (4) yacht
   (5) no error
2. (1) peculiar   (2) jeopardy   (3) forfiet   (4) respondent
   (5) no error
3. (1) bureau   (2) blamable   (3) desecration   (4) harass
   (5) no error
4. (1) falibility   (2) heinous   (3) myriad   (4) remnant
   (5) no error
5. (1) hygienic   (2) medallion   (3) midget   (4) prommisory
   (5) no error
6. (1) complacency   (2) efemeral   (3) exaggerate   (4) realize
   (5) no error
7. (1) lacquer   (2) currency   (3) exortation   (4) emolument
   (5) no error
8. (1) apologetic   (2) coroner   (3) clique   (4) exzema
   (5) no error
9. (1) disatisfied   (2) moribund   (3) warrant   (4) surgeon
   (5) no error
10. (1) defered   (2) extraordinary   (3) journal   (4) intercede
    (5) no error

# Commonly Misused Words

Many English words that sound alike are different in both spelling and meaning. These easily confused words are called *homonyms*. For example:

Lower back *pain* is a common ailment.
The school board recommended that the children who had broken the windows pay for each *pane* that had to be replaced.

The wooden *board* served as a temporary desk.
I'm always *bored* at our long staff meetings.

Other frequently misused words sound almost alike. For example:

Members of the council have agreed to *adopt* the proposal. (To adopt is to accept.)
To succeed, you have to *adapt* to new conditions easily. (To *adapt* is to adjust to change.)

The memo made an *allusion* to past product overruns. (An *allusion* is an indirect reference.)
The company is under the *illusion* that increased sales will improve its profit statement. (An *illusion* is an incorrect belief or perception.)

Finally, there are words that don't sound at all alike but whose meanings are often confused. For example:

If the bank decides to *lend* us money, we'll hire the personnel we need.
You may want to *borrow* from our library.

We were *eager* to begin the trip we had planned for more than a year.
(*eager* = impatient, enthusiastic, hopeful)
The child's parents were *anxious* about the diagnosis.
(*anxious* = worried)

In the following list, you'll find examples of correct usage for many commonly misused words.

1. accept — except

I *accept* at least one delivery each day.
Everyone *except* John left the meeting.

2. adapt — adopt

When visiting a foreign country, you must *adapt* to the local customs.
Our company plans to *adopt* a new sales program.

3. advice — advise

Because of Marla's excellent *advice*, Bob completed a successful business deal.
Marla *advised* Bob to be cautious.

4. affect — effect

The accident did not *affect* Thomas.
The *effect* on his brother, however, was great.

5. aggravate — annoy

Government spending *aggravates* the enormous deficit.
Having to leave my desk to find supplies *annoys* me.

6. all ready — already

Call me when the group is *all ready* to go.
By the time the guest of honor arrived, we had *already* finished dinner.

7. all right (*Alright* is not an acceptable word.)

   Is it *all right* to leave this window open?

8. all together — altogether

   The four of us were *all together* at the coffee shop.
   This book is *altogether* too long.

9. allude — refer

   In passing, the speaker *alluded* to the new technology in business.
   The speaker *referred* to statistics that demonstrated the rise of technology in business.

10. allusion — illusion

    I am amused at your *allusion* to my cooking as similar to fast food.
    You have the *illusion* that I enjoy that kind of music; I don't.

11. altar — alter

    The wedding group stood in front of the *altar*.
    Would it be inconvenient for you to *alter* your plans for this weekend?

12. among — between

    The campaign director divided the state *among* the *three* most competent assistants.
    The care of the children is often divided *between* the *two* parents.

13. amount — number

    You would not believe the *amount* of time I have spent on this project!
    I wish I could count the *number* of hours I spent.

14. angry at — angry with

    Ira was *angry at* the thought of working overtime.
    Ira was *angry with* his boss for insisting that Ira work overtime.

15. anxious — eager

    I am *anxious* about my child's illness.
    I am *eager* to see your new car.

16. as — like

Paula looks very much *like* her sister.
*As* it did last year, the radio station sponsored the debate.

17. ascend — ascent — assent

The aircraft *ascended* above the city.
The *ascent* to the tower was steep.
Because I value your opinion, I won't go ahead with the project without your *assent*.

18. awful — very — real — really

This fish tastes *awful*.
This fish tastes *very* bad.
Is this gold *real* or imitation?
Its shine is *really* bright.

19. because of — due to

*Because of* our tight budget, we're vacationing at home.
The increased enrollment is *due to* a renewed interest in vocational programs.

20. beside — besides

Linda sat *beside* Ellen in the cafeteria.
Who, *besides* Pam, is signed up for the company's exercise program?

21. born — borne

Our youngest child was *born* last month.
John has *borne* (carried) the burden by himself for long enough.

22. borrow from (*Borrow off* is unacceptable.)

Mickey *borrowed* the soldering iron *from* Allen.

23. borrow — lend — loan

May I *borrow* your pocket calculator?
I can *lend* you my mechanical pencil.
I need a $500 *loan*.

24. brake — break

I prefer a bicycle with a foot *brake*.
Because he did not *brake* in time, Herman crashed into the tree.
If you are not careful, you will *break* that dish.

25.  can — may

Some fortunate people *can* arrange their time to include work and pleasure.
(*can* = have the ability to)
You *may* park here only after 3 p.m.
(*may* = have permission to)

26.  capital — capitol — Capitol

Ricardo has 90 percent of the necessary *capital* for his new business venture.
Trenton is the *capital* of New Jersey.
New Jersey's *capitol* building is in Trenton.
Did you visit the *Capitol* when you were in Washington, D.C.?

27.  cite — sight — site

An attorney often *cites* previous cases to support an argument.
One of the most beautiful *sights* in the country is the Grand Canyon.
The alternative school will be built on this *site*.

28.  coarse — course

This *coarse* fabric makes my skin itch.
That is an acceptable *course* of action.

29.  complement — compliment

Bob's skills *complement* those of the rest of the department.
I'd like to *compliment* you for doing such a thorough job.

30.  continually — continuously

Tom is *continually* (frequently) late.
The alarm sounded *continuously* (without interruption) for ten minutes.

31.  council — counsel

Our neighbor has just been elected to the town *council*.
If you feel troubled, seek a friend's *counsel*.

32.  credible — creditable — credulous

Because the defendants had a good alibi, their story seemed *credible*.
As a result of many hours of hard work, Jane presented a *creditable* report.
You're too *credulous* — you shouldn't believe everything you hear!

34. currant — current

His unusual recipe called for *currant* jelly.
Because the *current* was swift, the canoe was difficult to maneuver.

35. desert — dessert

The *desert* is very hot and dry.
More and more soldiers have been *deserting* the army.
We had applesauce for *dessert*.

36. die — dye

Eventually, every living thing *dies*.
Blocking is a new way to *dye* fabric.

37. discover — invent

The builders *discovered* oil on our land.
Eli Whitney *invented* the cotton gin.

38. disinterested — uninterested

The *disinterested* observer of the accident was certain that the driver of the blue car was at fault.
Because I was *uninterested* in the lecture, I paid no attention.

39. draw — drawer

Marlene *draws* very well.
She keeps her art supplies in the top *drawer* of her desk.

40. emigration — immigration

The Harlows *emigrated* from England.
After *immigrating* to the United States, the Harlows settled in Kansas.

41. famous — infamous

One of the twins is a *famous* pianist.
The other, unfortunately, is an *infamous* car thief.

42. farther — further

My car can run *farther* on this brand of gasoline.
I cannot continue this discussion any *further*.

43. fewer — less

Gerry invited *fewer* people to her holiday party this year.
Since she moved from a house to an apartment, she has *less* space.

44. formally — formerly

Please dress *formally* for the wedding.
I was *formerly* employed by a jewelry company, but I am now working in a bank.

45. good — well

Murray has just gotten a *good* job.
Maria performed the job *well*.
Maria doesn't feel *well*. (*Well*, normally an adverb, is used as an adjective when it describes health.)

46. grate — great

The continuous harsh sound *grated* on my nerves.
A *grate* in the sidewalk covered the opening to the electrical wires.
Ernest Hemingway was considered a *great* writer in his own lifetime.

47. healthful — healthy

Orange juice is *healthful*.
If you eat properly and exercise sufficiently, you probably will be *healthy*.

48. imply — infer

Although he did not state it directly, the manager *implied* that we were losing business to the competition.
From the mayor's constructive suggestions, we *inferred* that she wanted the project completed as quickly as possible.

49. in — into

Marlene stood *in* the living room.
Pedro came rushing *into* the room.

50. it's — its

I think *it's* a fine idea!
The dog wagged *its* tail.

51.   kind of — sort of — type of
(These expressions can be used interchangeably. They should never be followed by *a*.)

   Mrs. Petrella always buys that *kind of* meat.
   I like that *sort of* book.
   This is my favorite *type of* record.

52.   later — latter

   Sue can finish the report *later* this week.
   I can meet you Tuesday or Thursday, but the *latter* would be more convenient.

53.   lead — led

   I'll need one more *lead* pipe to complete this plumbing job.
   I only enjoy a race when I am in the *lead*.
   John was unfamiliar with that route, so Jules *led* the way.

54.   learn — teach

   I am having difficulty *learning* how to use the word processor.
   Leslie is patiently trying to *teach* me how to use it.

55.   leave — let

   After the customs officer clears a traveler's baggage, the officer *lets* the traveler *leave* the area.

56.   loose — lose — loss

   Parents are usually excited about a child's first *loose* tooth.
   If you step out of line, you will *lose* your place.
   The company has recovered from last year's *loss* of profits.

57.   manor — manner

   The *manor*, or landed estate, dates back to feudal times in England.
   A pleasant *manner* is especially helpful for a salesperson.

58.   miner — minor

   The coal *miners* struck for better medical care.
   Many laws classify young people under eighteen as *minors*.

59.  moral — morale

   Because of Ed's high *moral* standards, he returned the wallet to its owner.
   The story of the boy who cried wolf has a *moral* that applies to everyone.
   Because the war was *immoral,* the *morale* of the troops was low.


60.  nauseated — nauseous

   When we drove past the skunk, the car was filled with a *nauseous* odor.
   The odor of the skunk *nauseated* Sara.


61.  pail — pale

   The paint is in one-gallon *pails.*
   Maria's long illness left her complexion *pale.*


62.  passed — past

   We *passed* the Model T on the parkway.
   Our profits increased by 17 percent during the *past* six months.


63.  peace — piece

   If we work together, perhaps we can achieve a lasting *peace.*
   I jotted down some notes on a *piece* of paper.


64.  persecute — prosecute

   Older children frequently *persecute* their younger brothers and sisters.
   If they violate the new law, they will be *prosecuted.*


65.  personal — personnel

   The items written in a diary are often highly *personal.*
   When applying for a job at a large company, you must go to the *personnel* office.


66.  plain — plane

   The meaning is quite *plain* and requires no further explanation.
   We rode for miles across the open *plains* of Kansas.
   The *plane* landed smoothly.
   Please *plane* that wood so that I can build a birdhouse with it.

67.   practicable — practical

Studying computer programming is a *practicable* plan for the future.
(*practicable* = workable, feasible)
The decision to computerize the payroll was a *practical* one that should help
lower our costs.
(*practical* = sensible)

68.   precede — proceed

A preface *precedes* the first chapter of a book.
Don't let me interrupt you; *proceed* with your work.

69.   principal — principle

A school is as good as its teachers and *principal*.
The *principal* actors in the play remained for a rehearsal of the second act.
The lever is the *principle* upon which many simple machines are based.

70.   quiet — quite

Find a *quiet* place where you can study.
That is *quite a* strong accusation.

71.   raise — rise

When we *raise* the flag, we'd like everyone in the audience to *rise*.

72.   sit — set

The committee members were asked to *sit* down.
Please *set* those papers on my desk.

73.   stationary — stationery

The price has remained *stationary*; it hasn't gone up or down.
We need a new logo for our business *stationery*.

74.   sure — surely

I am *sure* that Alice will be at the meeting.
You *surely* don't expect me to take notes.

75.   than — then

New York is smaller *than* Wyoming, but Wyoming has a much smaller
population *than* New York.
First the Eastern Seaboard was colonized; *then* settlers moved westward.

76.  their — there — they're

Employees can bring *their* children to the company's child-care center.
*There* must be an easier way to operate this machine.
As for the members of Congress, *they're* not always responsible for the wisest decisions.

77.  through — threw

The crew worked *through* the night to repair the wires.
When the Little League pitcher *threw* the ball, her teammates cheered.

78.  to — too — two

United States presidents often travel *to* foreign countries.
Many foreign heads of state visit the United States, *too*.
*Two* notable visitors were the late Anwar Sadat and Margaret Thatcher.

79.  vain — vane — vein

You're not usually *vain*; why do you keep looking at yourself in the mirror?
A rooster is the traditional weather *vane* symbol.
*Veins* carry deoxygenated blood to the heart.

80.  wade — weighed

The children *waded* near the shore.
The clerk *weighed* the fresh vegetables.

81.  waist — waste

It makes sense to measure your *waist* before you buy a pattern.
We talked about the dangers of chemical *waste* sites.

82.  weather — whether

What is the *weather* forecast for tomorrow?
*Whether* or not you wish to pay taxes, you must.

83.  who's — whose

The sergeant asked, "*Who's* responsible for clean-up today?"
Do you know *whose* turn it is?

84.  writes — rights — rites

Kurt Vonnegut *writes* excellent fiction.
Their attorney explained the family's *rights* in the lawsuit.
The religious *rites* of many Indian tribes are an impressive part of their culture.

85. your — you're

Where is *your* car parked?
*You're* doing a good job on the project.

# PRACTICE 16

Circle the number of the incorrect word in each paragraph. If there is no error, circle number 5.

1. Because I was <u>anxious</u> to avoid another argument, I <u>accepted</u>
   (1)                                                    (2)
   Roy's apology. Since his story seemed <u>credible</u>, there was no
   (3)
   point in carrying the argument any <u>further</u>. <u>No error</u>
   (4)        (5)

2. Carol left the elevator and <u>proceeded</u> to the <u>personal</u> office.
   (1)              (2)
   The unfriendly interviewer lowered Carol's <u>morale</u>, but she was
   (3)
   still <u>eager</u> to obtain the job. <u>No error</u>
   (4)                        (5)

3. The <u>effect</u> of the unusual visitor on the family was startling.
   (1)
   Mother <u>adopted</u> Mrs. Chuggley's speech habits; father <u>altered</u>
   (2)                                                        (3)
   his smoking habits to suit Mrs. Chuggley's allergy; and I found
   myself <u>continuously</u> saying, "Yes, ma'am." <u>No error</u>
   (4)                                      (5)

4. The <u>course</u> of action determined by the city <u>counsel</u> at its last
   (1)                                        (2)
   meeting has <u>already</u> begun to <u>affect</u> us. <u>No error</u>
   (3)              (4)        (5)

5. Family gatherings are always interesting. Grandpa is usually
   <u>angry with</u> Aunt Jean. Rhoda insists upon <u>sitting</u> <u>besides</u>
   (1)                                          (2)     (3)
   Grandma. Mother tries to divide her attention equally <u>among</u>
   all of the guests. <u>No error</u>                                   (4)
   (5)

6. I was <u>altogether</u> shocked when Sam returned the ice bucket he
    (1)

had <u>borrowed from</u> us last spring. When I <u>complemented</u> him
   (2)          (3)

for returning it so promptly, Sam's red face told me that he

understood my <u>implied</u> sarcasm. <u>No error</u>
    (4)      (5)

7. Please put the change <u>into</u> your pocket before you <u>lose</u> it. It's
        (1)        (2)

hard enough to keep pace with today's prices without carelessly

losing money. That <u>kind of</u> negligence makes me <u>loose</u> my
      (3)        (4)

temper. <u>No error</u>
   (5)

8. The <u>minor</u> <u>led</u> the team into the shaft. After several hours of
  (1) (2)

dangerous work, they <u>ascended</u> jubilantly. It had been a <u>really</u>
        (3)        (4)

terrifying experience. <u>No error</u>
     (5)

9. I am <u>formally</u> engaged in a program of good nutrition. I always
   (1)

eat a <u>healthy</u> breakfast. I consume <u>fewer</u> sweets and I spend <u>less</u>
  (2)      (3)     (4)

time stalking the refrigerator for snacks. <u>No error</u>
          (5)

10. Sue and her sister asked if they might go swimming at the pool.

Although both of them <u>can</u> swim <u>quite</u> well, <u>their</u> mother
       (1)   (2)   (3)

refused permission. Sue was very angry and said they were

being <u>prosecuted</u>. <u>No error</u>
  (4)   (5)

## PRACTICE 17

In each group, circle the number of the sentence that contains an
incorrectly used word. If there is no error, circle number 5.

1. (1) The damage has all ready been done.
 (2) Mr. Kelley was altogether too surprised to speak.
 (3) Events have borne out my prediction.

    (4) Perry is an altar boy at Queen of Peace Church.

    (5) No error

2.   (1) Please cite at least three examples.

    (2) The dealer was cited for contempt.

    (3) For that sight, we're planning a municipal parking lot.

    (4) When the bridge is within sight, look for our street.

    (5) No error

3.   (1) Was his work all right?

    (2) They ordered six yards of plain fabric and ten yards of plaid.

    (3) Do they have the capitol to invest?

    (4) Our club has fewer members this year than last year.

    (5) No error

4.   (1) I applied the brakes immediately.

    (2) Cars are borne across the river on a ferry.

    (3) Are you feeling all right?

    (4) When you are all ready, I will pick you up.

    (5) No error

5.   (1) Do the typing first; finish the filing latter.

    (2) The envoy was received formally at the ambassador's home.

    (3) Our department had a loss, but the rest of the firm did well.

    (4) We could hear a vigorous discussion of current problems.

    (5) No error

6.   (1) When you give your report, be sure to cite as many concrete examples as possible.

    (2) "I am surely not guilty of excessive spending!" he shouted.

    (3) The new copier was delivered through the basement.

    (4) Because of several miner disagreements, the discussion came to a halt.

    (5) No error

7.   (1) The consultant was asked to advise the planning board.

    (2) My advice is that construction of the bridge should be postponed.

    (3) She was hired because her experience would complement that of the rest of the staff.

    (4) Prospective homeowners are eager for reduction of the mortgage interest rate.

    (5) No error

8. (1) The attorney has placed the file for the Jones case in the bottom draw.
   (2) The senior citizen center will be formally opened next week.
   (3) Don't lose this pen; it is hard to replace.
   (4) Mike is quite an athlete.
   (5) No error

9. (1) We have passed the goal we set for the second quarter.
   (2) There was nothing to do but accept the plan.
   (3) I am opposed too airing family matters in public.
   (4) The crowd was quiet until the rocket ascended.
   (5) No error

10. (1) The manager was pleased that you had done such a creditable job.
    (2) No one knew him as I did.
    (3) Choose your coarse of action and stick to it.
    (4) I think the skirt is too loose on you.
    (5) No error

**PRACTICE 18**

Circle the error in each incorrect sentence. If there is no error, put a "C" next to the sentence. Write the correct word to replace each error.

1. Sam wants to lend your calculator for a few days. _____
2. Please contact me by phone. _____
3. The book alluded in great depth to the Civil War. _____
4. Company B's continued dumping of waste has aggravated the pollution problem. _____
5. His foot tapping really aggravates me. _____
6. Please rise your hand if you know the answer. _____
7. She gives the allusion of being much thinner than she is.

   _____
8. Bill sure doesn't want to work overtime. _____
9. John promised to learn Maria English. _____
10. George felt awful bad about the accident. _____

# Words and Phrases to Avoid

Some incorrect words and phrases are used frequently. Because we hear them so often, we may begin to think they are *correct*. No matter how frequently they are used, however, these expressions are not acceptable as proper English. In *My Fair*

*Lady,* Eliza Doolittle's dialect labeled her as "lower class"; the use of certain words and phrases can label us "uneducated." This may sound unfair, but most employers are looking for people who can give their businesses the best image. *Ain't* won't do it.

1. ain't

   We used to be able to say, "Ain't ain't in the dictionary." Now it is! Most educated people do not accept this word. You would do well to avoid it. *Ain't* is used incorrectly in place of *am not, is not, isn't, are not, aren't.*

2. could of

   This is incorrect usage. The correct term is *could have.*
   Example: I *could have* danced all night.

3. disregardless, irregardless

   These forms are incorrect. The word you want is *regardless.* Example: *Regardless* of the weather, I plan to wear my new suit.

4. graduate (high school or college)

   You did not *graduate* high school, you *graduated from* high school, or any other school.

5. anywhere (There is no such word as *anywheres.*)

   Marlene can't find her glasses *anywhere.*

6. nowheres

   This is incorrect usage. Use *nowhere.* Example: This debate is going *nowhere.*

7. off of

   Omit the word *of.* Example: He climbed *off* the bleachers.

## PRACTICE 19

Rewrite each sentence correctly.

1. This project is going nowheres.

   _____

2. He ain't a very good businessman.

   _____

3. Wilma could of had the promotion if she had wanted it.

   _____

4. Please take your feet off of my desk.

   _____

5. I graduated high school in 1979.

_____

6. Irregardless of your opinion, I plan to hire the person I interviewed Tuesday.

_____

# ANSWERS

## PRACTICE 1

1. malnutrition
2. coeducation
3. inappropriate (*or* misappropriate)
4. irreverent
5. impatient
6. illegal
7. misinform
8. unavailable
9. disassemble (*or* reassemble)
10. repay
11. depersonalize (*or* impersonalize)
12. acclimate

## PRACTICE 2

1. announcement
2. trying
3. snappiness
4. association
5. dispensable
6. definitely
7. economical
8. courageous
9. movable
10. heartily
11. practically
12. portable
13. rudeness
14. guidance
15. fulfillment

## PRACTICE 3

1. (4) irrational
2. (2) happiness
3. (4) misspell
4. (1) commencement
5. (1) safety
6. (5) No error
7. (3) accumulate
8. (4) noticeable
9. (2) argument
10. (5) No error

## PRACTICE 4

1. paint´ · er
2. pri´ · vate
3. of´ · fice
4. e · con´ · o · my
5. ad · vise´
6. bal´ · ance
7. dis · sat´ · is · fy
8. de · vel´ · op · ment
9. in · di · vid´ · u · al
10. pre · fer´
11. pref´ · er · ence
12. psy · chol´ · o · gy
13. vac´ · il · late
14. u · nan´ · i · mous
15. wretch´ · ed

## PRACTICE 5

1. (2) preference
2. (4) deterred
3. (5) No error
4. (3) deterrent
5. (4) occurrence

## PRACTICE 6

1. niece
2. deceive
3. thief
4. relieve
5. neigh
6. receive
7. conceive
8. belief
9. neither
10. seize

## PRACTICE 7

1. (2) mouthfuls
2. (1) Japanese
3. (2) sons-in-law
4. (5) No error
5. (1) wolves

## PRACTICE 8

1. (3) conclusively
2. (2) coronation
3. (1) similar
4. (2) achievement
5. (2) seize
6. (4) duped
7. (3) pertinent
8. (5) No error
9. (3) lovely
10. (5) No error

## PRACTICE 9

1. (5) No error
2. (2) merciful
3. (1) dissolution
4. (5) No error
5. (3) weird
6. (2) government
7. (3) cordially
8. (4) piece
9. (5) No error
10. (5) No error

## PRACTICE 10

1. (3) habitually
2. (4) appliance
3. (1) candies
4. (2) disappoint
5. (1) embargoes
6. (3) propelling
7. (4) truckfuls
8. (1) truly
9. (5) No error
10. (1) salaries

## PRACTICE 11

1. (3) niece
2. (4) relief
3. (3) referred
4. (3) assessment
5. (5) No error
6. (4) receipt
7. (1) acquired
8. (4) lieutenant
9. (1) adjournment
10. (1) carefully

## PRACTICE 12

1. (2) athletic
2. (3) temperature
3. (3) incessant
4. (1) legitimate
5. (5) No error
6. (5) No error
7. (5) No error
8. (4) tetanus
9. (5) No error
10. (1) fundamental

## PRACTICE 13

1. (5) No error
2. (1) absence
3. (3) discussion
4. (2) athletic
5. (5) No error
6. (1) Wednesday
7. (5) No error
8. (2) possession
9. (5) No error
10. (4) library

## PRACTICE 14

1. (2) aberration
2. (5) No error
3. (1) ascertain
4. (2) resilience
5. (5) No error
6. (3) lucrative
7. (4) surfeit
8. (1) wield
9. (5) No error
10. (1) psychology

## PRACTICE 15

1. (2) negligible
2. (3) forfeit
3. (5) No error
4. (1) fallibility
5. (4) promissory
6. (2) ephemeral
7. (3) exhortation
8. (4) eczema
9. (1) dissatisfied
10. (1) deferred

## PRACTICE 16

1. (1) eager
2. (2) personnel
3. (4) continually
4. (2) council
5. (3) beside
6. (3) complimented
7. (4) lose
8. (1) miner
9. (2) healthful
10. (4) persecuted

## PRACTICE 17

1. (1) already
2. (3) site
3. (3) capital
4. (5) No error
5. (1) later
6. (4) minor
7. (5) No error
8. (1) drawer
9. (3) to
10. (3) course

## PRACTICE 18

1. Sam wants to *borrow* your calculator for a few days.
2. Please *communicate with* me by phone.
3. The book referred to the Civil War in great depth.
4. C
5. His foot tapping really *annoys* me.
6. Please *raise* your hand if you know the answer.
7. She gives the *illusion* of being much thinner than she is.
8. Bill *surely* doesn't want to work overtime.
9. John promised to *teach* Maria English.
10. George felt *very* bad about the accident. *Or* George felt *really* bad about the accident.

## PRACTICE 19

1. This project is going *nowhere*.
2. He *isn't* a very good businessman.
3. Wilma *could have* had the promotion if she had wanted it.
4. Please take your feet *off* my desk.
5. I *graduated from* high school in 1979.
6. *Regardless* of your opinion, I plan to hire the person I interviewed Tuesday.

# 12.

# Developing Your Vocabulary

---

If you find when you sit down to write that words don't come readily, take heart. You are not alone in this problem. Many people have difficulty finding the right words to express their thoughts. The more words you have at your command, the more easily they will flow. General vocabulary development is an asset to anyone. Specific vocabulary development will help you with your particular writing needs.

## General Vocabulary Development

You may have heard it before, but this technique *is* valuable. Carry a small notebook with you. When you hear or read an unfamiliar word, jot it down. When you have time, look up the definition in the dictionary. If you are very ambitious, you can also look the word up in a thesaurus, or dictionary of synonyms. You may encounter synonyms you are already familiar with; knowing these words should make it easier for you to learn the new word.

But keeping a notebook of words and definitions will increase your vocabulary only minimally — unless you *use* the new words. In order to truly *own* a new vocabulary word, you must use it correctly. You may feel uncomfortable at first. It is interesting to note that few people are embarrassed to display a limited vocabulary. Many of us, however, are uncomfortable about appearing too smart. We don't want to offend others or to seem arrogant. Consequently, when we *can* say, "They *ostracize* people who disagree with their politics," we might instead choose, "They don't let in people who disagree with their politics." Get used to using your new words. Wear them proudly.

### Specific Vocabulary Development

Learn words that will help you with your personal writing needs. If you are a student, you need the broadest possible vocabulary. Have you been criticized for overusing a handful of descriptive words and verbs? Try the same techniques you used to collect general vocabulary: collect, define, use, and review. The texts and other books you read, the lectures you hear are all sources of new vocabulary.

Or perhaps, as a laboratory technician, you have to prepare monthly reports or write up the results of your experiments. If so, concentrate on learning the words and phrases that will help you explain your findings most clearly. Be sure to keep your audience in mind. Are your readers fellow scientists or a lay advisory board? Remember to develop a vocabulary that your audience will understand.

Are you responsible for writing grants or proposals? Learn the acceptable, appropriate terminology, but avoid becoming enmeshed in "jargonese."

Most businesses, professions, and school subjects have their own jargon, their own special vocabulary. Jargon has a specific meaning and, in fact, makes sense only in a particular context. Used properly this special vocabulary is acceptable. Certain words, however, seem to hold a particular attraction for many people who use the word in the wrong context. For example, you hear and see the word *interface,* which has a particular meaning in computer technology, misused regularly. An *interface* is a thing (a noun), an electrical gadget. Yet, it is used regularly as an action (a verb).

Correct:    Use a serial *interface* to connect the printer to your computer.
Incorrect:  The two committees will *interface* (meet) to compare their plans.

As you increase your vocabulary, therefore, remember to use special words in their proper places. A complete dictionary helps you do that by listing all the ways a word is defined. In addition, some dictionaries provide usage notes which discuss acceptable usage.

## Using the Dictionary

How often, when reading a novel, a magazine, a textbook, or even a letter, have you come across an unfamiliar word? Do you skip over it as though it never existed? Tell yourself you'll get back to it later and look it up? Write it down and plan to look it up? Or actually look it up?

Let us say you actually do look up the definition of the new word. Do you then assume you'll now remember it? Write it down to assist your memory? Write it down and occasionally review it? Or write it down, review it, and use it?

To help you develop a technique for expanding your vocabulary, try the following exercises.

### PRACTICE 1

For each word below, do the following:

(1) Guess. What do you think the word means? Write your definition.

(2) Look the word up in the dictionary and select one meaning, preferably the most common.

(3)   Write the dictionary definition of the word.

(4)   Write at least one synonym. Use a thesaurus if necessary.

(5)   Use the word in a sentence.

| | | |
|---|---|---|
| vanguard | emulate | adroit |
| articulate | ineluctable | prodigy |
| entrench | sanctimonious | access |
| enlightening | coveted | indictment |

## User-Friendly and Unfriendly Definitions

Learning to get the most from your dictionary takes practice. For instance, sometimes a dictionary defines a word by giving another form of the word itself. For example:

> intensity      the quality or condition of being *intense*.

Chances are, if you knew what *intense* meant, you would have been able to figure out what *intensity* meant. Often, of course, the dictionary will also provide more helpful definitions, such as *energy, strength, concentration* for *intensity*. But what if it doesn't? Then you'll have to look up the other form of the word — in this case, *intense*.

For most words, the dictionary offers more than one definition. Make certain that you select the definition that suits your use of the word. The dictionary also identifies parts of speech. It is helpful to know whether the word you want to use is a noun, a verb, an adjective, or an adverb. For example, you would not write, "John looked intense (*adj.*) at Mary." Correct usage would be, "John looked intensely (*adv.*) at Mary."

As you can see, most new words you learn come with a family. Consider your vocabulary development as similar to shopping at a sale: buy one, get two or three for free! Once you learn *intense,* for instance, you'll understand the meaning of *intensely, intensity,* and *intensive.* Now that's a bargain!

### PRACTICE 2

Select the correct word for each sentence below.

intense      intensely      intensive      intensity

1.   The _____ glare from the headlights made driving difficult.

2.   Phil works with such _____ that others have trouble working with him.

3.   As a result of _____ research, I found the exact information I needed.

4.   The state trooper pursued the hit-and-run driver _____.

## PRACTICE 3

Write your own sentences using the above forms of *intense*.

_____

_____

_____

_____

## PRACTICE 4

Select one of the following words to complete each sentence below.

extreme        extremist        extremity

1. Wear warm socks and gloves on your _____, or you'll get frostbite.
2. Tearing one's hair out is an _____ example of frustration.
3. Seen as an _____ in his isolationist beliefs, the senator was shunned.

# Using Context Clues

Have you noticed that people who read a great deal tend to have larger vocabularies? Reading gives you the opportunity to increase your vocabulary because often the words you don't know are surrounded by others you *do* know. The words and phrases that surround a word are called the *context*. Suppose, as you read the following paragraph, you don't know the meaning of the word *retain*. What context clues can help you unlock the meaning of this word?

All matter can be broken down into smaller units. The molecule is the smallest unit of matter that can exist independently and *retain* its chemical properties. Once a molecule is broken into smaller particles, or atoms, the chemical properties of the original substance do not necessarily remain.

After reading the passage, which of these words do you think is the correct definition of *retain:* (1) *change,* (2) *destroy,* (3) *keep* (4) *lose,* (5) *break*? The correct answer is number 3, *keep*. How did you reach that conclusion? Perhaps your thinking went like this: The paragraph says that a molecule is the smallest unit that can *retain* its chemical properties, or characteristics. On the other hand, if a molecule is broken down, these properties do not necessarily remain. This sentence suggests that until the molecule breaks down, it does *keep*, or *retain*, its chemical properties. Thus you can guess that *retain* means "keep."

## PRACTICE 5

Use context clues to help you select the correct definition for the italicized word in each paragraph.

1. In recent years there has been a great emphasis on the high-technology professions. Numerous students have been trained for these positions, usually considered the "wave of the future." Some educators are concerned, however, that the tide will run out before those students currently riding the wave reach the shore — or the job market. Several decades ago the trend in education was to counsel most students to become teachers. During the 1960s, there was a *glut* on the market, and many trained teachers were forced to seek other fields of employment. Will the 1990s bring a *glut* of people trained to work in high-tech fields?

   *Glut* means (1) employment; (2) economy; (3) excess; (4) earnings; (5) demand.

2. The public has become increasingly aware of the dangers *posed* by chemical waste. At one time, no one questioned an industry's right to manufacture products and to dispose of wastes as it saw fit. Today, just as nonsmokers demand "breathing space" from smokers, many citizens are holding neighboring industries responsible for keeping the air and water clean.

   *Posed* means (1) modeled; (2) asked; (3) presented; (4) hidden; (5) covered up.

3. Work is the salvation of some and the *bane* of others. While scores of people scurry to their offices eager for the day's work, just as many reluctantly trudge to work as though going to jail. The right kind of job can provide satisfaction. Sometimes, though, we require incentives beyond the job itself, incentives such as the need to support a family or to pay for our education.

   *Bane* means (1) savings; (2) love; (3) reluctance; (4) motivation; (5) ruin.

# Using Word Parts

Finally, you can improve your vocabulary by examining the structure of words to see how they are formed. The main part of a word is called the *root* (for instance, *write*). To that we can add prefixes to the beginning (*re*write) and suffixes to the end (writ*er*). By learning common roots, prefixes, and suffixes, you can increase your understanding of the meanings of words. Many roots are taken from Latin and Greek words. Review these common prefixes:

| Prefix | Meaning | Usage |
|---|---|---|
| pre = | before | This manuscript *predates* the Bible. |
| in = | not | The work is still *incomplete*. |
| im = | not | It will be *impossible* to finish it on time. |
| dis = | not | Many people *dislike* working overtime. |
| ex= | out of | *Excommunication* is a severe penalty. |
| un = | not | Right now, earning a Ph.D. is an *unrealistic* goal. |
| a = | outside of, not | January's low productivity was *atypical* for our firm. |
| auto = | self, same | Have you read Margaret Mead's *auto-biography*? |
| re = | again | The new tenant wants us to *redesign* the first floor. |
| mal = | bad | One more *malfunction* and I am getting rid of this computer! |
| il = | not | A major problem in our society is *illiteracy*. |
| ir = | not | These blouses are inexpensive because they are *irregular*. |
| co = | with | Marisol has requested our *cooperation*. |
| mis = | wrong | The child was scolded for *misbehavior*. |

And here are some helpful root words:

| Root | Origin | Meaning | Usage Example |
|---|---|---|---|
| tekne | Greek | skill | You can't always transfer the newest scientific *technology* to a commercial product. |
| alere | Latin | to nourish | In the digestive process, food passes through the *alimentary* canal. |
| putare | Latin | to think | The flow chart describes how we *compute* the average of the class's grades. |
| videre | Latin | to see | Are you comfortable looking at a *video* display screen? |

| dominium | Latin | property | Include your *domicile,* or legal residence, on that form. |
| bene | Latin | well | The program will *benefit* my favorite charity. |
| dicere | Latin | to say | The office manager would always *dictate* his letters and memos in the afternoon, when the office was quieter. |
| facere | Latin | to do, make | The company assembles the product at their newest *factory.* |
| votens | Latin | wishing | Supposedly, attending the meeting was *voluntary.* |
| unus | Latin | one, single | Our common goals for the company *unite* us. |
| signum | Latin | sign | The flashing light we saw was a *signal* of the ship's arrival. |
| portare | Latin | to carry | I don't intend missing the game; I'm going to take a *portable* television set with me. |
| manu | Latin | by hand | On that machine, *manual* mode means that the operator must turn it on and off. |
| ferre | Latin | to bear, carry | Mildred Jackson accepted a *transfer* to the Chicago office. |
| ducore | Latin | to lead | The exocrine glands discharge their fluids through *ducts.* |
| scribere | Latin | to write | Because we have a word processor now, you won't have to interpret what I *scribble.* |

Now here are some common suffixes:

| Suffix | Meaning | Usage |
| --- | --- | --- |
| = ness | state of | John expressed happiness at his promotion. |
| = ly | every, like | Please review these reports carefully. |
| = ous | full of, having | If this product is successful, we could become famous. |
| = able | able, capable | I find Mr. Cord's offer reasonable. |
| = ive | forms adjectives or nouns from verbs | Maria is our most creative writer. |
| = ance | forms nouns from verbs or adjectives | After your injury, I understand your reluctance to play on the company team. |
| = ment | state of | This establishment has a fine reputation. |
| = ion | condition of | Carlos is the newest member of our organization. |
| =al | pertaining to | Dr. Wilenski does not consider this a practical move. |
| = ful | characterized by | Please be tactful when you refuse his help. |
| = er | doer | The plant hired another welder. |
| = or | doer | Doris is the creator of these sculptures. |

**PRACTICE 6**

Complete the following sentences by adding a prefix or suffix to the italicized word in each. In some cases, you will have to make minor spelling changes.

1. The sudden appearance of the dark shadow    *mobilized* the frightened child.
2. Because the testimony was    *relevant*, the judge ordered it stricken from the record.
3. If you are always complaining, you will earn the title of office    *content*.
4. You must understand my    *ease* at competing with you for this position.
5. While supplies are *plenty*    , I don't mind lending them to other departments.
6. Even Agatha Christie would not have    *covered* the cause of that fire.
7. Unless we invest in *educate*    , our entire society will lose.
8. John has a record of all deposits, but no record of the *disburse*    of funds.
9. I give up; I find this problem    *solvable*.
10. A committee of interested citizens decided to    *store* the town hall that had been built in 1805.

# ANSWERS

## PRACTICE 1

These sentences are suggestions, of course. Your sentences will differ, but make sure your usage is correct.

vanguard        the foremost position in an army, fleet, or movement (n.)
(forefront)

       Gloria Steinem has always been in the *vanguard* of the women's movement.

articulate        able to speak clearly and eloquently (adj.)
(eloquent–adj.        to speak clearly; to express ideas well (v.)
say–v.)

       William is the most *articulate* speaker on the debating team.
       If you can't *articulate* what you mean, your listeners may find your ideas confusing.

entrench        to fix securely, to establish (v.)
(establish)

       The squirrels are firmly *entrenched* in our attic.

enlightening        informative, educational, clarifying (adj.)
(informative)

       Dr. Garcia's lecture about everyday activities that pollute was *enlightening*.

emulate        to try to equal or exceed; to imitate (v.)
(copy)

       Martin Luther King was a great leader whom young people would do well to *emulate*.

ineluctable        not to be avoided or overcome; inevitable (adj.)
(inevitable)

       Although we knew what to expect, we watched the soap opera to learn the *ineluctable* fate of the heroine.

sanctimonious        pretending to be righteous; hypocritical (adj.)
(hypocritical)

       *Sanctimonious* political candidates may make moving speeches calling for aid to the needy and then do nothing for them after Election Day.

coveted        highly desirable or sought after (adj.)
(desirable)

       The Olympic athletes competed for the *coveted* medals.

adroit        skillful, deft (adj.)
(skillful)

       Although John seemed to be an *adroit* politician, he lost the election.

prodigy        an expert; one with exceptional talents (n.)
(expert)

       Michelle had been with the company only a year, but her work earned her the reputation of *prodigy* of the laboratory staff.

access        approach, pathway (n.)
(passageway)

       Those homes are being torn down to provide an *access* route to the new highway.

indictment        accusation, charges (n.)
(disapproval)

       The supervisor's critical memo was clearly an *indictment* of the assistant's behavior.

## PRACTICE 2

1. The *intense* glare from the headlights made driving difficult.
2. Phil works with such *intensity* that others have trouble working with him.
3. As a result of intensive research, I found the exact information I needed.
4. The state trooper pursued the hit-and-run driver *intensely*.

## PRACTICE 3

Answers will vary.

## PRACTICE 4

1. Wear warm socks and gloves on your *extremities,* or you'll get frostbite.
2. Tearing one's hair out is an *extreme* example of frustration.
3. Seen as an *extremist* in his isolationist beliefs, the senator was shunned.

## PRACTICE 5

1. (3) excess
2. (3) presented
3. (5) ruin

## PRACTICE 6

1. immobilized
2. irrelevant
3. malcontent
4. unease
5. plentiful
6. uncovered
7. education
8. disbursement
9. unsolvable
10. restore

# 13.
# Assessing Your Writing Skills

Apply all the skills you've learned in *Writing the Easy Way* as you work your way through the practice exercises in this chapter.

## PRACTICE 1

Edit these paragraphs. Look for errors in grammar, punctuation, spelling, capitalization, and word usage. Then check your answers against the answer key at the end of the chapter.

1.  In this century, chemistry has been involved in playing a part in the studying of the life sciences. As a result of this, there has been, increasingly, a coming together of the research going on in chemistry with the other sciences. Increasing knowledge as far as complex chemical structures are concerned, is helping scientists to understand basic life processes. This is the area of biochemistry — a bringing together of biology and chemistry.

2.  At that time, the United States, too, had their own ideology that they based their expansion on during the mid-eighteenth century. It was called "Manifest Destiny." Literally, Manifest Destiny means, "a future event accepted as inevitible." During the Polk era of the 1840s, Manifest Destiny was the belief that the Americans fate was to live in and posess North America and that the country would be a place of freedom of religion, democracy, republicanism and Anglo-Saxonism.

3.  Here is an account of the Texas controversy. In the Louisiana purchase of 1803, the U.S. obtained the title to Texas from France, which they later passed on to Spain in the Adams-Onis Agreement of 1819 in return for Florida. In the same year, Moses Austin was granted a grant of land from Spain to settle a colony in Texas. His son, under a newly created Mexican government, independent of Spain, established a colony between the Brazos and Colorado rivers.

4.                 Public Relations Announcement

    The company's supervisor of operations states, "if a customer has a problem relative to our machinery, I get the call direct. With our direct contact with our representatives all over the Country, I can make the necessary delivery and repairing is also a possibility. Our sales people are like family. There just as anxious to affect the needed change as we are. Customers appreciate that.

5.   Sometimes personal learning needs are not met by existing curriculum. So independent study can be another facet of the Adult College Plan. This gives the student an option. That is to create a study program tailored to their needs.

    Classes are held in the evening. That way students are still able to work at their jobs during the day. They also can use their work as a laboratory. Here they blend theory and practice under supervision. They also earn credit for it.

## PRACTICE 2

Rewrite the following letter correctly. There are errors in form, grammar, capitalization, and punctuation.

Martin Rivera
Well-Built Construction Company
21 Warren Road
San Francisco, CA 90042

Dear Mr. Rivera,

    You had been highly recommended by my neighbor but I fail to see why. A three-day project ends up taking two Weeks. Your workmen left my yard a shambles after building a garage for me. I ask the men to clean up their garbage but they refused. Please have someone from well-built complete this clean-up within the next five days. Thank-you.

                        sincerely,

                        Wilma Jones
                        San Francisco, CA 90042

## PRACTICE 3

Rewrite the following memo correctly. There are errors in form, grammar, capitalization, spelling, and punctuation.

MEMO

FROM: Jane Smith

TO:     Lisa Manning

About our 1985 annual sales conference. Im assembling my presentation to the sales representatives but I find I'll need some audio-visuals — can you get me a large screen, slide projector, and a lighted pointer. Also, the sound system at last years Conference is inadequate for the size room we had. Will you be able to improve on that this time?

Let's meat about 2 week's before the conference and go over the points I'll be covering, in case you have some particular products you want covering in depth.

## PRACTICE 4

Change the tone of the following letter by replacing the italicized words with words from the list below. You will have to change "a" to "an" in some cases.

| | | | |
|---|---|---|---|
| inferior | received | recently | quality |
| extremely | request | appear | |

249 Lenox Avenue
Cranford, New Jersey 07076
March 7, 1985

Mr. John Rainier, President
World Wide Distributors
400 North Avenue
Westfield, New Jersey 07090

Dear Mr. Rainier:

I *just got* your package and must say I was *very* disappointed. You had promised me a *good* product, and I received a *junky* one. How can such a well-known company *come-off* to be reputable and yet make such an unreliable item? I respectfully *ask for* a refund.

Sincerely,

James Worth

## PRACTICE 5

Correct the word usage errors in the following sentences. Note: Every sentence has an error.
1. I will contact you in the morning.
2. Please except my apology.
3. Jim doesn't want to argue. He said to leave it be.
4. Ms. Atler did not intend her comments to infer that you were incompetent.
5. Please carry your résumé to the Personal Department.
6. Any good report clearly states the principle issues.
7. Salad and fresh bread make a healthy lunch.
8. When Mr. Smith wants your advise, he will certainly ask for it.
9. We have less people to accommodate.

10. You sure don't think that I could type that quickly, do you?
11. This is a whole nother topic.
12. I found last year's seminar more valuable then this year's.
13. Mr. Wilson came in the meeting room 45 minutes late.
14. The choice for best composition is between these four.
15. That's the kind of a book I can relate to.
16. There are less people in line for the 6:40 show than there are for the 8:40.
17. Many people are becoming concerned about the affects of air pollution on our health.
18. Winston tastes good, like a cigarette should.
19. José cannot find that position paper anywheres.
20. Its not too late to cancel the plane reservations.


## PRACTICE 6

Rewrite the following letter correctly. There are errors in form, grammar, capitalization, spelling, and punctuation.


April 2 1984
Mr. Melvin Appley
27 Main Street
Smalltown, USA 00000


Arthur Johnson, Superintendent of Schools
110 Pine Street
Smalltown, USA 00000


Dear Superintendent Johnson,

I would like to take this opportunity to say that I am in receipt of and have read your report on raising eligibility standards for high school athltes which you reported to our school. My argument against higher academic standards for athltes centers around the fact that a student can pass from grade to grade with a 1.5 average but they can't play football. Hows that fair?

I'm not saying that it's not true that the first job of any student in school should be academic. I'm just saying you can't say "that no one without a 3.0 average can participate in sports." That doesn't take into account special students needs or abilities. Also, a students' educational experience should be as complete as possible, it should include the interaction that takes place in sports. Please reconsider your position in this matter.

Sincerely,

Melvin Appley

## PRACTICE 7

Correct the following communication. Look for spelling, punctuation, and grammar errors. Simplify the sentences whenever you can. In brief, apply all that you have learned about effective communication.

### Report To Stockholders

Comparing our company's productivity to our Japanese counterpart, in the 1970s, it increased by 20 percent and, at the same time, in that period of time, Japan's production grew over 100 precent. Likewise our German competitors which had productivity levels higher than ours were also less than Japan's. Still we must remember that although our industry still has the highest productivity in the world. Other countries, however, and especially Japan, has gained in productivity so consistantly every year so that by the end of the 1970s these foreign rivals were now in a position to invade our markets and they took away a lot of our business. They did this by beating us not only in price but also their quality has been consistently better.

Can Universal Widget corporation reverse this trend in the 1980s? Your Board of Directors thinks it is capable of doing so. Universal Widget corporation has adapted a leadership position in research and development which will allow us to innovate, it will bring the newest and most advanced widget to the marketplace. In addition, because our plants are completely computerized, they are able to bring our product to the market place faster and it's also a better product.

# ANSWERS

## PRACTICE 1

1. In this century, chemistry has played a part in studying the life sciences. As a result, research in chemistry has come together with research in other sciences. Increasing knowledge of chemical structures, for example, helps scientists understand basic life processes. This cooperation has resulted in biochemistry, bringing together biology and chemistry.

2. During the mid-eighteenth century, the United States, too, had its own ideology on which to base its expansion. The ideology found its roots in the theory of "Manifest Destiny." Literally, Manifest Destiny means, "a future event accepted as inevitable." During the Polk era of the 1840s, Americans believed it was their fate to live in and possess North America, and it was the country's fate to be a place of freedom, of religion, of democracy, and of republicanism.

3. In the Louisiana Purchase of 1803, the United States obtained the title to Texas from France, and the Texas controversy took shape. The United States passed the title on to Spain in the Adams-Onis Agreement of 1819 in return for Florida. In the same year, Moses Austin was granted land from Spain to settle a colony in Texas. Austin's son, under a newly created Mexican government, independent of Spain, established a colony between the Brazos and Colorado rivers.

4. Public Relations Announcement

   The company's supervisor of operations states, "If a customer has a problem with our machinery, I receive the call. Through direct communication with our representatives all over the country, I can make the necessary deliveries and repairs. Our sales people are like family. They are just as eager to effect the needed changes as we are. Customers appreciate that."

5. Existing curriculum does not always meet personal learning needs. The Adult College, therefore, offers students independent study as another facet of its plan. Students, then, have another option: to create a study program tailored to their needs.

   Because classes are held in the evening, students are still able to work at their jobs. In addition, students use their work as a laboratory, blending theory and practice under supervision and earning credit for their efforts.

## PRACTICE 2

All underscored portions are corrections.

1409 Grange Lane<br>San Francisco, California 90042<br>June 30, 1985

Mr. Martin Rivera
Well-Built Construction Company
21 Warren Road
San Francisco, California 90042

Dear Mr. Rivera:
    You had been highly recommended by my neighbor, but I fail to see why. A three-day project ended up taking two weeks. Your workmen left my yard a shambles after building a garage for me. I asked the men to clean up their garbage, but they refused. Please have someone from Well-Built complete this clean-up within the next five days. Thank-you.

Sincerely,<br>Wilma Jones

## PRACTICE 3

All underscored portions are corrections.

TO:     Lisa Manning, Sales Manager

FROM:  Jane Smith, New Product Development Coordinator

DATE:  December 19, 1984

RE:     1985 Annual Sales Conference

I'm assembling my presentation to the sales representatives, but I find I'll need some audio-visuals. Can you get me a large screen, a slide projector, and a lighted pointer? Also, the sound system at last year's conference was inadequate for the size room we had. Will you be able to improve on that this time? Let's meet about 2 weeks before the conference and go over the points I'll be covering, in case you have some particular products you want to cover in depth.

## PRACTICE 4

We've shown only the body of the letter here, with the corrections as you should have made them.

I *recently received* your package and must say I was *extremely* disappointed. You had promised me a *quality* product and I received an *inferior* one. How can such a well-known company *appear* to be reputable and yet make such an unreliable item? I respectfully *request* a refund.

## PRACTICE 5

1.  I will *call* (communicate with) you in the morning. (Contact means *touch*. It is widely misused.)
2.  Please *accept* my apology.
3.  Jim doesn't want to argue. He said to *let* it be.
4.  Ms. Atler did not intend her comments to *imply* that you were incompetent.
5.  Please carry your résumé to the *Personnel* Department.
6.  Any good report clearly states the *principal* issues.
7.  Salad and fresh bread make a *healthful* lunch.
8.  When Mr. Smith wants your *advice,* he will certainly ask for it.
9.  We have *fewer* people to accommodate.
10. You *surely* don't think that I could type that quickly, do you?
11. This is a whole *other* topic.
12. I found last year's seminar more valuable *than* this year's.
13. Mr. Wilson came *into* the meeting room 45 minutes late.
14. The choice for best composition is *among* these four. (One chooses *between two* items and from *among three* or more.)
15. That's the *sort of* book I can relate to.
16. There are *fewer* people in line for the 6:40 show than there are for the 8:40. (*Fewer* refers to number; *less* refers to amount.)
17. Many people are becoming concerned about the *effects* of air pollution on our health.
18. Winston tastes good, *as* a cigarette should.
19. José cannot find that position paper *anywhere*.
20. *It's* not too late to cancel the plane reservations.

## PRACTICE 6

Answers will vary.

27 Main Street
Smalltown, USA 00000
April 2, 1984

Arthur Johnson, Superintendent of Schools
110 Pine Street
Smalltown, USA 00000

Dear Superintendent Johnson:

I have read your report to the school committee on raising eligibility standards for high school athletes, and I disagree. Since other students can pass from grade to grade with a 1.5 average, how fair is it to insist that athletes maintain a 3.0 average? A student can move from grade 9 to grade 13, but he can't play football.

I agree that the first job of any student should be academic work. You can't declare, however, that only students with a 3.0 average can participate in sports, because that requirement doesn't take into account the needs or abilities of special students. In addition, a student's educational experience should be as complete as possible. The interaction that takes place in sports is a part of that experience. Please reconsider your position.

Sincerely,

Melvin Appley

## PRACTICE 7

In the 1970s, our company's productivity increased 20 percent in comparison to our Japanese counterpart's increase of over 100 percent. In the same years, our German competitor's productivity, while less than the Japanese, also increased more than ours. Although our industry still maintains the highest productivity in the world, our foreign competitors have shown more consistent gains each year. By the end of the 1970s, therefore, our foreign rivals had invaded our markets and taken away a substantial amount of our business, beating us not only in price, but also in quality.

Can Universal Widget Corporation reverse the trend in the 1980s? Your Board of Directors thinks the company is capable of doing so. Universal Widget Corporation has adopted a leadership position in research and development which will allow us to innovate, bringing the most advanced widget to the marketplace. In addition, our newly computerized plant can produce a better widget and can bring it to the marketplace faster.

# Resources

*The American Heritage Dictionary of the English Language.* Boston: Houghton Mifflin, 1970.

*The American Heritage Dictionary of the English Language, New College Edition.* Boston: Houghton Mifflin, 1978.

Ammon-Wexler, J., and Katherine Carmel. *How to Create a Winning Proposal.* Santa Cruz, California: Mercury Communications, 1976.

Bernstein, Theodore M. *The Careful Writer: A Modern Guide to English Usage.* New York: Atheneum, 1973.

Blumenthal, Lassor. *Successful Business Writing.* New York: Grosset & Dunlap, 1976.

Elsbree, Langdon, and Frederick Bracher. *Heath's Brief Handbook of Usage.* 9th ed. Boston: D. C. Heath & Co., 1977.

Flech, Rudolph. *How to Write, Speak and Think More Effectively.* New York: Harper & Row, 1960.

Follett, Wilson. *Modern American Usage: A Guide.* Edited and completed by Jacques Barzun and others. New York: Hill & Wang, 1966.

Fowler, H. W. *A Dictionary of Modern English Usage.* 2nd ed. rev. by Sir Ernst Gowers. New York: Oxford University Press, 1965.

Hart, Archibald. *Twelve Ways to Build a Vocabulary.* New York: Barnes & Noble, 1967.

Hochheiser, Robert M. *Throw Away Your Résumé!* Woodbury, N.Y.: Barron's Educational Series, Inc., 1982.

Lefferts, Robert. *Getting a Grant.* Englewood Cliffs, N.J.: Prentice-Hall, 1978.

Mack, Karen, and Eric Skjei. *Overcoming Writing Blocks.* Los Angeles: J. P. Tarcher Inc., 1979.

*A Manual of Style.* 12th ed., rev. Chicago: University of Chicago Press, 1974.

Mersand, J., and F. Griffith. *Spelling the Easy Way.* Woodbury, N.Y.: Barron's Educational Series, Inc., 1982.

Mersand, J., and F. Griffith. *Spelling Your Way to Success.* Woodbury, N.Y.: Barron's Educational Series, Inc., 1982.

Miller, Casey, and Kate Swift. *The Handbook of Non-sexist Writing*. New York: Lippincott & Crowell, 1980.

Oliu, Walter E., Charles T. Brusaw, and Gerald J. Alred. *Writing That Works*. New York: St. Martin's Press, 1980.

*The Random House Dictionary of the English Language*. Unabridged ed. New York: Random House, 1967.

Strunk, William, and E. B. White. *The Elements of Style*. 2nd ed. New York: Macmillan, 1972.

Turabian, Kate L. *A Manual for Writers of Term Papers, Theses, and Dissertations*. 4th ed. Chicago: University of Chicago Press, 1973.

*The U.S. Government Printing Office Style Manual*. rev. ed. 1973.

*Webster's Secretarial Handbook*. 2nd ed. Springfield, Mass.: Merriam-Webster Inc., 1983.

Wilson, Robert F., and Adele Lewis. *Résumés for Executives and Professionals*. Woodbury, N.Y.: Barron's Educational Series, Inc., 1983.